The Most Phenomenal Book You'll Ever Read About...

WOMEN

Secrets Most Guys Don't Know About Women:

A Man's Guide to Understanding Women

Written By

The Minister Of Manhood

"A Woman Wants To Get Your Time, Without Giving Up Her Pussy, A Man Wants To Get Her Pussy, Without Giving Up His Time."

-Patrice O'Neal

unless with written permission from the publisher. All rights reserved.

The information provided herein is stated to be truthful and consistent, in that any liability, in terms of inattention or otherwise, by any usage or abuse of any policies, processes, or directions contained within is the solitary and utter responsibility of the recipient reader.

Under no circumstances will any legal responsibility or blame be held against the publisher for any reparation, damages, or monetary loss due to the information herein, either directly or indirectly. Respective authors own all copyrights not held by the publisher.

The information herein is offered for informational purposes solely, and is universal as so. The presentation of the information is without contract or any type of guarantee assurance.

The trademarks that are used are without any consent, and the publication of the trademark is without permission or backing by the trademark owner. All trademarks and brands within this book are for clarifying purposes only and are then owned by the owners themselves, not affiliated with this document.

Table Of Contents

The Female Mindset

The Energetic Feminine Role Of A Woman

A woman secure, safe and comfortable in her feminine energy and all that comes with being a woman is naturally nurturing, caring, spiritually intelligent and emotionally intuitive. The feminine energy a woman possesses allows her to become healers, empaths, psychics, nurturers and teachers of the children because they are emotionally intuitive by nature.

Their sensitive nature allows them to feel the energy of others easily. Women are the bridge to the spiritual realm and they have the power to feel very easily what isn't seen or felt by the unaware man. But in the modern day with feminism and toxic femininity now exposing so many women to more masculine energy than ever, she's become much more masculine, tough and distant from her true feminine gifts.

A woman that embraces her feminine energy and gifts can help a man connect his mind to his heart. That's because a woman represents the heart as man represents the head or mind. A man in his masculine energy is extremely logical, analytical and facts driven. But a woman in her feminine energy is extremely emotional, intuitive and feelings driven. Together they compliment each other by connecting the heart and mind of a man.

And a man in his masculine energy helps a woman organize her emotional mind into a much more focused and powerful laser of the mind and heart of a woman. For example just like the act of sex and then childbirth in the physical realm, in the spiritual realm the woman takes the spiritual seed from a man's mind and becomes the spiritual vessel that brings the souls into the world.

The woman and man together in their rightful energetic functions are extremely powerful beings when they embrace their energetic and physical roles on earth. But because the mindset of the modern woman doesn't understand her feminine energy she craves the strength she sees a man possess to will his creativity onto the physical world.

She envies a man's ability to manifest his desires, and be the one in charge of creating all of the physical ideas that she enjoys. So she loses sight of her creative ability and gifts to manifest spiritually. Instead of embracing what it is to be a woman, she desires to be the head of everything in her life.

She desires the ability to control everything and do what a man does. But it is her desire to be a man, do wha a man does and be better than a man that creates an energetic imbalance between the man and the woman in the modern day. Instead of working with a man to manifest both of their desires together, she wants to be the provider, the protector and the creator of everything in her own life, by herself.

This is why so many women have become extremely masculine energetically. This is also why so many women that a man meets today in the dating markets are tired, unhappy, anxious, burdened and angry with the pressure of physical life. The physical life and the manifestation of it alone was never her job to perfume by herself.

Much of her wrong thinking has taken root from recently becoming a target of the social media, feminist, the entertainment industry, the beauty industry and the materialism propaganda machine that has consumed her mind with external desires. She has now adopted the mindset that what she has, what people think of her and who she becomes is more important than anything in life. Does this sound familiar?

Does this sound like the ego centered, success focused, greed based and desire for recognition and power driven mentality of a man? Of course it does! All of these traits are natural to a man because nature built him to provide. If a man wasn't focused on getting as much food, power and social status in the tribe his family wouldn't eat or be protected from male and animal predators.

The primal mentality of a man is based upon mother natures basic law, only the strong survive and the weak die. Watch a nature show and you'll quickly see that mother nature will always set that standard as rule #1. But for a woman her role and her mind naturally has been set differently. The woman is the nurturer, the grower and the protector only when she has to be.

Just approach a baby in the wild and see who the first is to run up. The father of course! Men and women in the modern society are out of their natural energetic balance and order. Because when a woman decides to act like a man and a man starts acting like a woman everything gets confusing and the children suffer the most.

For a society to function naturally just like in mother nature, the men and women must stay in their natural order because they both have an important but opposite part to play in the survival of the human species. All you have to do is look at a man and woman physically, mentally, energetically and biologically to see that they are opposite, yet both human.

A man gets the most respect from a woman and the world when he is in the role of a man. And a woman gets the most respect and admiration from a man and the world when she is in the role of a woman. They are both extremely powerful in their different ways because they have access to their natural gifts given to them energetically.

She doesn't have to go out into the world and demand equality from a man. All she has to do is understand that she is not a man and can never truly become a man or get what a man gets. But a woman who is a feminine caring, nurturing, resourceful, sensual, intelligent, wise, and good at being a woman gets benefits that a man doesn't get access to in the world also.

There will never be equality in benefits between a man and woman. Both men and women get benefits that each other won't have access to regardless of how much they want them. Because if women really wanted equality then they would have to give up the benefits that they get as being women that men don't get also.

This would mean that women would also have to give up the double standards that benefit them also. This is why for a woman who truly loves being a woman, the fight should never to be better than or equal to a man, but to become the best woman that she can be. Only then does she will get the highest benefits of being a woman in which a man will never have access to.

Men and women are equal in their importance in the universe, but the fact is that they will never be equal in benefits. Men and women are both given different skills that compliment each other. If they weren't different energetically and biologically from each other then there would be no energetic space between them to create attraction.

It is the seductive shape of a woman, her mentality, the energy of her sexuality, the emotion of a woman's vulnerability and her nurturing capabilities that makes her attractive to a man. When the man and woman accepts and then embraces their individual energetic gifts they can then works together as a team.

If they embrace the strengths, gifts and benefits that each other gets as being a man and a woman they are unstoppable. This is when things energetically, mentally and emotionally balance out for both of them. And now the individual burdens of the world they carried alone are now lifted.

Because the pressure of survival is shared equally in ways they are individually built to handle they can get much further in life. But when they are off balanced and in competition they only stagnate their own physical, spiritual and mental progress in life. This is why so many women and men are burnt out on life.

They're both trying to carry the burdens of the physical world alone because of being hurt by each other. Hurt has led them to believe the feminist and alpha agenda that they're better off alone. That somehow being alone is better than working together with each other to build something for themselves, their children and for the benefit of the society as a whole.

Just as the sun and the moon share the same sky yet have two different purposes, man and woman are built to be together not separate. Mother Nature is always showing us the natural order of things, but often men and women aren't open to listen. As a deeper example, let's look at energetic roles of the sun and the moon.

The sun represents the masculine energy and the moon represents the feminine energy. The role of the sun is that it radiates light in the form of solar energy that make is possible for the physical life on this planet to exist on earth. The sun is the strongest and most powerful force in our galaxy. Simply just let it get extremely hot and sit outside and see how long you last.

The power of the sun will eventually either push you to go find shelter from it or it will take your life if you stay in it long enough. The sun drives weather, ocean currents, seasons and makes plant life possible through photosynthesis. Without the strength of the suns heat and light, life on earth would not exist.

The sun gives life to all of the things we see and rely on in the physical world. The Moon controls the energies that we cannot see but can feel which is in reference to the spiritual world. It gives migration cycles to the animals, earths magnetic field, determines the circadian rhythm of time, fertility cycles and birth rates.

The moon makes the earth livable by stabilizing the climate, and moderates the tides of the water that creates a hypnotic rhythm that has guided humans since their time on earth. They are both different but both very important and necessary for life to exist. Everything on planet earth would be off balance for life to exist if the sun wanted to be the moon, or if the moon wanted to be the sun.

True equality means that both energies are free to be their natural masculine and feminine energetic selves. Not ever to be or do what the other one does. This is where modern feminist ideas have only hurt women energetically and thrown them off balance.
Equity is what women truly need in the physical world, not equality.

The word equity means that both men and women have a natural right to the same fairness of treatment and justice regardless of their masculine or feminine energies. But the more a woman wants to equal to a man the masculine she becomes. The more masculine a woman becomes the more unattractive energetically she becomes for a man who is totally in his rightful place as masculine energy.

She's completely un attractive mentally for a man because masculine energy is competitive by nature. A man doesn't want to compete with a woman that he wants to make his wife. Attraction is created through the opposite energies of the masculine energy and the feminine energy desiring to feel their energetic opposite.

A masculine man will always be attracted naturally to a feminine woman without thought. This energetic connection and attraction goes both ways. A masculine woman wants a masculine man but because he is repelled by her tough and hard energy, she often finds herself with a feminine man.

Even in a gay relationship energetically there is a more masculine energy partner, just like there is a more feminine energy partner. Have you ever seen a stud or a femme male? You can see clearly which energy they internally embrace. Regardless of their born sexual origins if they are more masculine or feminine they desire their energetic opposite.

This is just the way that mother nature works. If you put two magnets of the same pole close to each other they will repel each other. The major reason why so many modern masculine energetic women can't find love is because so many women have become like men energetically and mentally. So naturally it repels the masculine energy in men they desire.

You'll often hear a masculine woman say that she wants a strong, powerful, accomplished and masculine man, but she doesn't understand her energy or mother nature at its core. Her desire for a masculine man shows her ignorance of natures laws. She doesn't want or desire to energetically embrace her role as a woman so why would a man desire another masculine energy?

Why would he want to mate with a masculine woman when his internal nature desires his feminine energetic opposite? That doesn't mean he won't have sex with a masculine woman. She can attract a masculine man with her external looks, but he won't stay with her long term because she's too competitive and combative mentally due to her masculine energy.

If a woman wants to find a mate in the world she shouldn't want to compete with a man's energy, she should desire to complete with a man's energy that's the difference. A woman's natural order is to spiritually and emotionally nurture the growth of the physical world the man created. A woman is perfectly built to beautify and maximize the potential of what he has built.

Just go to a masculine man's house and a feminine woman's house to see the difference. Masculine, tough, strong and powerful men built the blueprint and laid the concrete of that house with other men. But when she put her gifts to beautify and make a house a home there is no competition between her and a man. Her ability to pay attention to the details of the house are far superior.

The decorations, the smell, the feel, and the cleanliness of the house are so much better than his. This is what a masculine man cannot do without the help of a feminine partner in his life. When a woman is fully in her feminine energy, a woman allows a man to escape his logical mind and connect more with his heart.

A man cannot become fully enlightened until he learns to connect his heart and mind together as one. The heart and mind connection of a man leads him into using his masculine energy to lead, build, protect, grow and create for the benefit of himself and those he loves. This is why there's nobody more important in a masculine mans heart than his mom.

But this is dependent upon if he had a mom in her feminine energy or not of course. Just as the sun grows the life on the planet, the moon nurtures it and gives it the time they need to rest. That's because the feminine energy of the moon is there to balance out the powerful masculine energy of the sun. Too much sun would kill everything.

When the energy of the man and woman's masculine and feminine energy are one they now have full access to their divinity physically and spirituality. This is how babies, galaxies and worlds are built. Feminism causes women to think that her giving birth means that she makes the babies, which is completely wrong.

She is the shelter from the elements that the baby needs to grow once the mans seed is planted until it's ready to blossom. Just like if you planted a seed in the soil of mother earth. The plant doesn't grow immediately and it would never grow if you just set it out in the sun because it would dry out and shrivel up to become useless.

So when the woman understands her place in the cycle of life and the man also understands his, harmony is the energetic result. But when a woman fights her energetic role on planet earth, all hell breaks loose as we see happening today.

Understanding Feminine Energy

Feminine energy is simply the expression of the right brain hemisphere. This means it's more than just a woman's mind, it's a universal mind of feminine energy that makes up who she is. The left brain and the right brain have two different functions and they also have two different thinking styles that govern their beliefs and decisions.

The right brain is responsible for emotions and feelings. The right brain is able to take in everything that's happening around it and process it all at once. This process is called synthesis. Feminine right brain energy is the creative energy. This is where ideas and creativity come from. The right brain is also where seduction and eroticism stems from.

This is the side of the brain responsible for sensuality and where the emotion of seduction is driven from. This is the natural state of a feminine woman. This is why a woman who is not seductive, sensual, creative and emotional is not in her feminine right brain energy. She is out of her natural energetic order and in her masculine and protective energy.

When a woman is in her masculine state it is often the result of hurt and pain. Something she's been through in her life caused her pain. And the energy of that painful experience hides within her to keep her in a protective, guarded and masculine state.

Because she's in her masculine energy she is guarded, combative and it's extremely hard for her to be vulnerable out of her fear of experiencing more hurt and pain. She is operating from her energetic masculine side, which is her left brain. So she isn't open or vulnerable enough to experience true love and passion with a masculine man.

Because passion and sex is a right brain function. Passion is the natural and pure expression of the feminine right brain energy. High level creativity is all born from the right brain feminine energy. Deep feelings and emotions are right brain, while intuition is a result of a deep feminine energy connection within herself.

Finding a naturally feminine, vulnerable and friendly woman is hard enough to find in today's modern culture. That's because so many women would rather protect themselves with masculine energy, instead of using her feminine energy to heal herself. Often she has no understanding of her feminine energy enough to know how or where to even start the healing process.

Her rejection of the older women in her life who could teach her has hurt the modern woman tremendously. She looks down on the women of old. And sees her grandmothers, mothers and great grandmothers as weak and old fashioned in their beliefs. So she doesn't see why being with a man could benefit her more than being the modern independent woman.

So as a man it's vital that you understand at least the basis of where her thinking comes from, so you understand the women you'll be dealing with in the dating marketplace. The modern energetically masculine woman is built to rebel against you. But the feminine woman is built to complement you, not compete with you. This is the difference between the two.

And if you meet with any woman regardless of how attractive she is that wants to compete with you, then you gotta let her go quickly. She is not wife or mother of your children material and you cannot change her into it. Because feminine energy is wife energy and masculine energy is competition energy.

You can't build anything of value with a woman that's competing against you because her goal is to win against your energy. She's looking to compete with you, just like you compete with another man at sports. She wants to ultimately destroy you by defeating your will to win. She only wants to win and that means that you have to lose in the process.

Look around and you will see the effects of the defeated men who dealt with masculine women who destroyed their confidence, their manhood and their will to win in life. These masculine women only want to compete with a man, not cooperate with him. It makes her ego feel good to see your confidence levels diminish and your will to stand up for yourself against her fade.

These women are what can be referred to as "man eaters". She'll never want to cooperate and win together with you. She's not energetically aligned with a man to enjoy helping him, so in turn she enjoys helping to destroy him. Your woman is supposed to be the opposite of that. A feminine energy woman wants to build with you.

She wants to be aligned with you and be focused on a common goal so you both can win together, that's a wife.

Feminine energy is at its best when it compliments and stimulates a man's masculinity. When her energy makes you feel stronger, smarter and more secure, not insecure. So gauge the women you meet by her energy and you will increase your odds of finding a wife.

The Feminine Vs The Masculine Woman

A **Masculine** Woman is a mentally, emotionally and or physically hurt woman who becomes naturally very protective of her emotions and vulnerabilities.

1. She is hard in her heart from pain her mind is set in its old ways of thinking

2. She has a lot of trust issues and emotional baggage from past failed relationships

3. She's lost hope in men and the ideal fairy tale of love, loyalty and romance altogether

4. She's become disillusioned and burnt out on life and a positive future for herself

5. She keeps a very closed mind to any new positive suggestions and can't grow because she's stuck emotionally

Avoid closed minded women set in her ways you can't teach. You don't even want to try and teach an old dog, new tricks, just get a new dog. Why would you ever desire to fight with any woman to listen to your ideas and suggestions?

It's easier to teach someone that's willing to learn, than to unteach something that's already been taught. The mind will always fight for its old beliefs over the new beliefs because they learned their old beliefs first. It's called cognitive dissonance.

A **Feminine** Woman is open to suggestion, lighter about life and eager to learn new things because she hasn't had a lot of negative experience with different men.

1. Her mind is fresh and open to new ideas that would benefit both of your lives for the better

2. She still has hope for the future and she still possesses passion, fun and living for the moment

3. She enjoys making you happy and looks to please you instead of only focusing on what pleases her

4. She knows that she becomes more valuable to a man that sees her as irreplaceable

You can only grow with a woman who is open to new suggestions. Her mind has to be open, then she will be open to the plan you give her. The mind of a feminine woman is fertile ground to the man that plants seeds in her fertile ground. If you plants the seeds of success in her, reward her desires and pick women with feminine energy, you'll ultimately reap a good harvest.

Those seeds will harvest a great mother, friend, partner, wife and a successful feminine woman. But with a masculine woman her mind isn't fertile ground. Its dry, brittle, hard, lacks the sufficient nutrients, infertile and not capable of reaping a harvest. She's mentally to stuck in her past emotionally as the role of a victim to grow any new thoughts, beliefs and ideas.

Everyone else is to blame for her negative and masculine mentality. She isn't ready to take full responsibility for letting go of the past so she can move forward in life. Her healing when she comes to the realization that life is hard for everybody. The only thing that we control is our reaction to the hard times that come.

We can change our outcomes if we change our perception about what happened to us in the past. Even if it was an extremely negative experience, there's always a lesson in it. That means that she'll have to move forward and move on, not hold on. The more she holds onto the pain of the past the more it takes a toll on her energetically until she lets it go.

A woman's energy tells you some very simple clues to where she's at emotionally. That's why it's incredibly important as a man to see past her body and look into her to feel her vibration. When you gain a woman in your life, you get much more than her body, you get her mind. And either her mind comes into in your life as a gold mine or as a land mine.

Miss Right Vs Miss Gotta Be "Right"

The Power Of The Right Woman In A Mans Life

A man can unlock certain powers, characteristics and magnetic energies within himself, his mind and his masculine energy when he has the "right" woman in his life. But he loses access or never gets access to those same masculine powers, characteristics and magnetic energies when he has misses gotta be "right" in his life.

There's a big difference between the minds and powers of these two types of women. The right woman for a man has an inner wisdom that upgrades a man's ability to tap into his highest potential because she adds to his life. She unlocks his heart and it's in his heart where a new source of wisdom, knowledge and understanding exists.

She can help to sharpen his logic because she will say and do things for a man that's focused on his best interest. And when she says and does these things that enhance his confidence, character and masculine energy he becomes a more powerful man. The right woman in a man's life has a unique and amazing gift to give him.

But the miss have to be "right" woman in a man's life has curse words and difficulties for a man. When she's the right woman for you she's feminine, soft and in touch with her emotional self. She knows how to plant the seeds of thought into your mind without force or conflict. She knows how to gently guide you into understanding and wisdom.

But the always have to be "right" woman only knows how to guide a man through force and conflict. She tries to force you into understanding through anger and manipulation instead of through love and tenderness. Avoid the miss always have to be right because she will torment, complicate and bring a headache to your life because she likes to fight.

Fighting and conflict is an addiction to these women because she'll try to force a man to listen. And the woman who loves to fight isn't focused on the bigger pictures of your vision, her only focus is on winning. She won't stop fighting and forcing you to accept her opinions until you submit, even if she's wrong.

This is a prime example of a toxic woman and toxic femininity. That's because she will lic, manipulate and even twist your words just so that she can justify in her head doing things that ruin the relationship. Then when the relationship is over it will always be your fault that the relationship died.

She'll never admit her wrongs or accept that her need to fight to be right instead of listening was the true reason the relationship couldn't survive. For any man there's no winning with these types of women because she loves to talk more than she loves to listen. And a woman who can't listen as much as she talks becomes a man's mental and physical prison.

Because even when the relationship is over she'll be determined to ruin your name and your reputation by spreading lies, exaggerations and excuses to why "you" were the problem. She will never take responsibility for her actions in the relationship. As a man it's your job to listen and watch how she talks much more than how her body moves when she walks.

When a woman can't hold her tongue when it's time to listen then she doesn't have discipline of the tongue. And a woman who doesn't have discipline of the tongue not only does she not listen to instruction, she'll use her tongue to create conflicts with you and other men in the world. Men everyday get killed due to fights that miss have be "right" got them in to.

All because she had to speak up when it wasn't necessary. She just couldn't let go and cool off when someone did something that she didn't like. She had to respond to her urge to fight out of her need and desire for conflict. These types of women are to be avoided at all costs.

Always with any woman you meet check her receptivity. Does she have the desire to listen when you talk? If so then that's a sign of her respect for you. When a woman respects you she'll listen, but if she doesn't she wont. For a woman to listen and respect your words even if she disagrees gently she has the gift of patience. This is a huge attribute of a worthy woman and potential mother of a man's children.

Your job is to look for miss right in your life because she will become the light in your life. She will enhance your masculine powers and enhance your ability to attract success in your life. But miss have to be "right" will repel people, opportunities, positive energy and inevitably bring you conflict, disagreements and pain.

For a man to grow he needs a woman who desires growth also. But miss always have to be right will always be stuck and keep you stuck also. As soon as you try to get ahead in life she'll bring you back further than you've progressed out of her disdain and inner lack of respect for you.

"Avoiding a fight is a mark of honor, only fools insist on quarreling." -Proverbs 20:3

Women Love, "Love" Not You

Women are not in love with the idea that most men think of "love" as. For men love is an action, and for women love is a feeling. This means that men and women not only love differently but see "love" in two very different and opposite ways. A man sees love in a very tangible way as in what he does for her is a display of his love.

But a woman sees love in a very intangible way as in how he makes her feel and how she feels about his love is "love" to her. So a woman's love is based upon her own perceptions about what he does for her. Her love is internal and extremely easily influenced by her control and not his. This is why so many men truly have no idea in their relationships how their women truly feel.

A man thinks by him doing acts of love for her that it's going to be enough to keep her love, but it's not. A man can give his woman everything that she wants and be an amazing guy who listens to her problems and shows up when she needs him to, but her love for him could still change because it's not based upon him.

It's based upon hormones in her brain. Women are in love with the internal "feelings" they call love that are in reality love hormones and not the actual actions of love as a man thinks. These internal feelings in the brain are caused by at least 2 "love" hormones named oxytocin and dopamine.

Sure he can do things to stimulate these hormones in her brain occasionally, but after a while the same actions create less releases of these "love" hormones in her brain. Also how she feels about the man trying to stimulate these "love" hormones is a big factor. She felt this "love" high with every new man she was in a relationship with especially in the "honeymoon phase".

This is why the honey moon phase was so easy. Every time you did something for her the release of love hormones were at its peak. But over time her brain released less and less of these hormones especially as she got used to you and what you do for her. This is why when the relationship goes bad she says I'm not in love with you anymore.

All this simply means is that you don't make her feel the "love" hormone anymore. You don't inspire dopamine releases in her brain that "feeling" anymore when she sees you after missing your presence like it did earlier in the relationship. Ultimately the reality of the situation is that her "love" feelings for you have faded and you don't stimulate her brain anymore.

You don't excite her anymore and she craves that "love feeling" again. So she leaves you or goes out into the world to look for the man that makes her "feel love" again. And once she finds him she finds herself after some time not "feeling love" for the next guy anymore also. So the cycle only continues after multiple failed relationships but she doesn't understand why.

She doesn't understand why there's no "good men" in the world and believes that it's the men instead of her "love" chemical addiction. She takes on the victim role and uses the men that she left in her path as the ones to blame for her lack of relationship success. But the truth is that she doesn't understand herself or her own female human biology.

She doesn't understand that what she feels is "love" never was the actual and factual describable actions of love. She was just in love with feelings, and not people. That's why she could sleep with your best friend while you're together and say that you don't make her feel "happy" or "loved" anymore.

She is chemically and hormonally driven by the brain as men and women all are. But the difference is when it comes to "love", men and women are just wired differently. It wasn't always personal, it was just he made her feel the high and excitement of that "love" feeling again for a moment.

She can blame revenge or your lack of loving her for cheating, but in her search for a hormonal high the bigger picture and who she hurt wasn't her concern. Her concern was to please herself with a new "love" high that was too hard for her will power to resist. This is why it's so important as a man to stay tapped into the energy and the actions of a woman.

You must always pay attention not to her facial expressions when you do something for her, but be paying attention to her energy when it happens. This is your master key to her true mindset. Because when she changes what she thinks of you and how she feels about what you do for her, her love feelings leave soon after.

Because her love is chemically and hormonally based upon her perception of you and what you do for her, a woman's feelings of "love" changes immediately when her mind changes. And her changed feelings will always change the relationship. Her love is extremely fickle and based upon her internal judgement of you.

If you move wrong in a way that turns her off on you and her together, her loves gone. And there's nothing you can do to turn her love back on without her help. Her feelings of love for you and her together will change at the drop of a dime. And any false move on your behalf, will change her feelings of love towards you altogether.

And once a woman's feelings of "love" for you dissipate, she'll begin looking for the next man who makes her feel that "love" again. This is why she can say confusing things like "I love you, but I'm not in love with you anymore." Love alone can't be built upon "love" hormones alone.

Because then your relationship with her is built upon an easily changeable and quickly fleeting emotion. You have to build a relationship with a woman based upon facts and not feelings because feelings change, facts don't. This means that you have to talk about what she specifically needs to feel love so that she has to hold herself accountable to that standard.

She can't say later in the relationship that she doesn't "feel" love for you anymore based upon floating ideas in her head. She has to make them real to her so that she can't use her feelings as an excuse to leave a good relationship with a great man. Making her tell you what she needs to feel loved will force her to deal with reality and not the illusion of love.

This means that if she says certain things make her feel loved and if you do them, there's no excuse for her to use you as a reason to leave. And if she decides to leave the relationship she now has to take full responsibility for not accepting your love actions and now she's the problem, not you.

And if you did what she said makes her feel love, it's now her problem she changed how she felt. The better looking she is and the more pictures she has of herself on the internet, the more "love" chemical options she has available to her. This keeps her from having the ability the focus seriously on any one single long term relationship fully.

This is because she has become programmed from the social media algorithm to feel the emotional and physical highs of new likes and new attention. So it's extremely difficult for her not to cheat or to want to feel that "feeling" again. It's like a drug user whose first high is amazing.

But the issue is every single time that they do that drug after that it will never be as euphoric as the first time that high released the dopamine in their brain. The drug user will need more and more of the drug over time just to be satisfied with the high. The same goes for good looking women, models and social media addicts.

The more highs she gets from likes, loves, dm's and male attention the more she needs. Because so many women are flooded with "love" chemicals constantly on social media they have become even more hardwired to live their everyday lives based upon feelings and not facts. They now pursue external validation more than a purpose or principle like class, sophistication or having wifely skills.

They chase the highs of likes, fame, validation and male sexual attention more than they chase solid relationships with good men. This is why the amount of promiscuous women in this society has grown exponentially. Now showing your attractiveness to the public for attention and internet fame has became so much more frequent in this day and age.

So as a man don't confuse her intimacy, her sex or her confessions of love for you with her commitment. She can give you her body while another man has her mind. That's because she's always loved the feelings of "love" and not you. She's in love with the high of "love". And like a drug abuser chasing the next high, she will chase the high of "love" over everything.

Because to her that high means her happiness. Now when you hear a woman say "I left you because I needed to find my happiness" or "I love you, but I'm not in love with you anymore" you'll understand what she really meant. You don't get her high anymore and she had to find the next "love" high with a new man.

The Mindset Of A Ho

A ho has built up such a high tolerance of "love" highs by having sex with so many different men, that she only gets small doses from each men she sleeps with now. But because of her internal issues like depression or trauma, sex is her drug of choice. Like a repetitive drug user not even sex gives her the high it used to, but it still makes her feel wanted and attractive.

Even in this vicious cycle of sexual pleasure she's still only looking to get the high from the release of oxytocin and dopamine primarily. Because her desire to get high off of the power from feeling attractive and wanted, and her need to run from her personal traumas, she isn't afraid to be forward in her way of talk or in her way of dress to attract sexual partners.

Because she's had so much sexual contact it doesn't bring the same high to her as a woman who doesn't get to experience so many different men. This is often what makes her act emotionally numb to men. Because of how easy it is for her to manipulate a man sexually she sees men as weak.

She thinks that she's winning the game in her mind because she's beating men at their own game and getting what she wants out of them. But they're getting what they wanted out of her also. And she doesn't truly understand that being a girl who is emotionally led is playing a logical man's game.

This sex game she's playing is extremely dangerous to her mind, her body and her future. This is why so many women are damaged emotionally today. Mentally and physically men are different. By her giving up what men want the most for free or for little value she always loses because she loses her ability to pair bond with a good man.

She loses her shame and her dignity because she says brash and sexually perverted things that would be sacred to her and a good man. She shows and says in public that which would be best suited for her and her partner in private. You can easily recognize a ho in public because she doesn't have a problem speaking openly about sex.

Because it's a topic she enjoys talking about and likes to talk about often. She knows that sex is the topic most men want to talk about. And by talking about sex she will get other mens sexual attention very quickly. Her comfort level talking about sex is due to her high number of sexual experiences with men.

She may be sexually advanced in bed and understand what a man wants sexually, but she really has no idea what a man wants or desires mentally from a woman. Most ho's don't know how to relate to a man other than sexually, because she isn't confident in her mental or intellectual abilities.

Getting a mans sexual attention is easy, but keeping his mental and emotional attention takes intelligence on her part. She knows a man wants sex but doesn't know what else he wants. And because she doesn't want to put in the hard work to find out, she uses her feminine seduction and flattery to get his sexual attention, validation and approval instead.

A ho can't truly relate to a man spiritually, emotionally or mentally because internally she's untrusting and angry at many of the men she's slept with for never staying because she truly wanted them to stay with her. So she never experiences higher levels of love and compassion with a man.

All because she doesn't understand that a woman is in charge of giving a man sex, but a man is in charge of giving a woman a relationship. Giving a man sex won't make him stay. In the long run giving away her sex so easily without creating a bond with a man only makes her unworthy of a real relationship with a good man.

She's just given herself away to so many men that she can't connect to a man more than physically. Dealing with a ho or sexually promiscuous woman is much different than dealing with a woman who has only been with a couple of men in her past. A girl with little experience is a lot more delicate in how she deals with men.

That's how a man knows the difference between the two. A ho is loud, brash and easy to show her private parts to the public. But a woman who isn't sexually as experienced with men has more shame. So she's much more comfortable keeping her privacy. Once you understand the difference you'll understand that playing with a ho is like playing with fire.

Not only do you connect with her physically, you connect to her spiritually and emotionally. You take on her emotions when you put your dick inside of her and you take on her spiritual energy when you exchange sexual energy with her. Not only do you put your body at risk you put your soul at risk. So see dealing with a ho in any way as danger!

How To Know If Your Girl Is Easy

#1. She Enjoys Time With Guys More Than Girls

She says things like "I don't have any girlfriends" or Girls don't like me" then that's a red flag. When she has different "guy" friends she hangs out all the time with without having you around that's another red flag.

#2. She Always Tries To Get The Attention Of Your Friends

When other men come around she gets extra talkative and friendly to them more than you. This means that she likes to be the center of attention especially when other men are around. Some women are addicted to male attention and they get stimulated mentally and physically when men other than you are around. Especially new and attractive men that she doesn't know.

#3. She's Slept With Someone In Your Friend Circle

Easy women use sex as a weapon. This is why she will sleep with someone you know or admire to get revenge on you. Or she'll sleep with multiple friends in a group, knowing it's going to cause problems in the friend circle. Your girlfriend or wife shouldn't be hanging around you and your friends. She has to always guard herself against what another man wants because a man will always test her, even your friends.

#4. She Parties All The Time And Every Weekend

She has to go out on the weekends with her girls or else it's an argument. These types of women have developed the unhealthy idea that having a good time is only hanging around a bunch of other people partying and drinking. Any woman who wants to drink all the time is already a woman who is destined to make moral and ethical mistakes with her body. Alcohol lowers a persons inhibitions and ability to make the "right" decisions in the moment.

#5. She Knows Everyone, Everywhere, Especially Men

Everywhere you go there's another random man she knows that you have never seen before. And then she's always approaching these men or getting approached by these men for hugs. She never gets approached by women or very rarely compared to how many guys approach her. When you ask her about these men, she always says that they're just "friends" or people she grew up with.

#6. She's Always In Another Mans Face

She's always in another mans face or groups of men talking or listening to them instead of you. And you never really see her talking to other women, only other men. This is a sign that she's attracted to the guy or she always needs a lot of male validation. She's showing that she enjoys being liked by other men than you. This shows that the type of woman you have is addicted to attention, especially from men.

It's only a matter of time until one man says the right words and then talks her out of her panties. She likes being liked by all men, even if she doesn't like him in return. Just being liked, admired and desired sexually makes her feel good inside. And places like clubs and bars are easy places to get male sexual attention.

#7. She's "Extra" Friendly With Men All The Time

She's the first to say "hi" to everyone always even when it's unnecessary. This means that she's internally needy and wants to be approved by everyone. So to get this attention she's extra outgoing and forward with everyone always. There's no reason for a woman to be "extra" friendly to other men when she has a committed man.

Extra friendliness is a girls go to sign to show a man that she's interested. And she would be very upset if you were "extra" friendly to other women. That's because she knows that extra friendliness is how a girl shows a man her interest in him. Even if she's not interested in him, she wants him to desire her.

The Dangers Of Her Ho Phase

When a woman hits puberty, she experiences a biological urge to have sex. This is the nature in a woman telling her that she is ready and able to mate. They call this feeling horny or horniness, but really it's her hormones giving her body and mind chemical instructions. The hormones present in the body are there to give our body instructions.

The feminine nature is to accept and receive the seed of a man. So her body is telling her that it is time for her eggs which she is now producing in her body to receive the sperm of a man to fertilize the egg she has waiting inside of her. This is no different than a female dog or cat "in heat". The difference is male dogs and cats do not go into heat once they start making sperm.

They can fertilize any egg whenever they're given the opportunity to. Because this urge to mate is so strong in her, she becomes highly sexually active and then calls it the "ho" phase. Simply because biologically most women don't understand their own bodies. Her body yearns to be penetrated sexually so anytime she's horny she looks for a sexual partner to fulfill those desires.

Because of her horniness she'll put herself at risk by having sex with men she's attracted to sexually, but not likely mentally. But often a woman doesn't understand her internal sexual urges enough to consider the dangers to her body, her mind or the energy of her womb.

She doesn't understand that once she lets a man enter her body sexually, there is now a sexual imprinting that happens inside of her. So when a young man enters a female he not only puts his penis inside of her, he inserts his energy into her. She doesn't understand what's happening other than the feelings that the sexual acts gives her.

But the body knows and understands on a deeper level what's happening. What's happening is that her body is calling for a males instruction. Her body is calling for the masculine principle of leadership. Her body wants to be given the seed from a man so it can fulfill its purpose to nurture that seed.

The seed a man gives into a woman is no different than the seed someone decides to plant into the ground. The ground doesn't grow anything without a seed being planted first. The seed is filled with the instruction within it that tells it exactly what it is meant to grow. This is why an apple seed grows an apple instead of a watermelon.

Genetically and energetically they are made up of two different energies. The ground simply serves as the protection that the seed needs to grow. And it feeds the seed the nutrients it needs to feed it as it grows. The seed is the man's sperm and the ground is the woman's eggs and then her stomach. But energetically and genetically each mans seed is different.

So if the instructions inside of the seed were to grow a baby and the energy of the mental environment of a man is toxic and of a low energetic vibration, her womb is imprinted with the same low vibratory energy. This is why often after the "heat" phase of her life she ended up directionless and lost after she had children with these low vibratory men.

Or after the sex the relationship went badly it traumatized her from that point on. She's traumatized because she had sex with a low vibration man who energetically imprinted her body. And she had sex with a man without the ability to lead a woman into anywhere but the bed. But now her body is still looking for male direction even as an adult.

And to prove this fact, most of the occupations she takes on are either working for men or working for male attention as in strip clubs, porn, only fans, etc. This understanding that a woman craves male leadership, admiration and attention is what social media websites have capitalized on and built billion dollar businesses based upon.

They have built billion dollar businesses based upon her desire to make herself look pretty so that she can take attractive pictures of herself to get male attention. She doesn't take pictures solely so other women can say how beautiful she is. She wants women to say how beautiful she is to assure her that she has the ability to be attractive enough to get male attention and hopefully his direction.

This is and has always been the purpose of marriage. Even the seed of a man's sperm is filled with genetic information and instructions for the egg to become. Can the egg create a child without the male sperms instructions? Of course not. Most women don't understand the science of her womb. She doesn't understand the spiritual and scientific process that is taking place inside of her womb.

So in the early stages of her body craving a mans seed she abuses it through random sex with men who are not mentally, sexually or energetically suited to imprint her body with the male leadership that she truly needs. So when a woman has sex with a man during her ho phase with underdeveloped men her womb then craves the energy and instruction of an underdeveloped man.

This is why so many women crave the energy of the "bad boy." In reality he's just a young and underdeveloped man mentally and energetically that she's attracted to sexually because he's immature like she is. But because she has no understanding of how sex with random and immature men affects her body in the long run she damages her womb.

Instead of older women teaching her the errors of their ways they let their daughters make the same mistakes.

They embrace the ho phase themselves to excuse their behaviors to avoid the guilt present that's a result of the errors in their early judgement of male sexual partners. So many women will act as they embrace the ho phase as a part of being a young girl, but this is an example of toxic femininity.

Toxic femininity is defined as the negative behaviors a woman does that she excuses to avoid moral responsibility. Because instead of teaching other young girls the impact that random sex has had on her life, she excuses the toxic mindset that every girl has a ho phase. And teaches young girls that it's acceptable, not detrimental to her future.

But it is dangerous and damaging to a young girls mind, her body and her future to accept that the ho phase is a normal and very acceptable part of being a woman. Instead they should be taught the power that a man has to imprint her energetically in this time of her life. And that the energy of the men that she sleeps with at this age carries through the rest of her entire life. Now lets go deeper on exactly how.

Why A Woman's Body Count Matters

Women like to say that a man not wanting a woman with a lot of sexual experiences is about a man's sexual and mental insecurity but that's incredibly wrong, uneducated and a blatant double standard. In reality there's mental, physical and spiritual effects that result from a woman having too many sexual partners and sexual experiences in her past.

In reality too many partners make her a highly unsuitable mate for a man looking for a wife. A woman who has too many sexual partners in her past is a huge red flag and cannot be taken seriously for a serious man looking to partner. Because she's already displaying the basic psychological signs of a damaged self esteem and need for external approval.

This can be a result of sexual trauma like past sexual abuse, rape, incest or very early exposure to sexual influences. It can also be a result of an inadequate childhood due to parenting mistakes or lack of parenting influences altogether. Somewhere mentally she's showing her neediness for the approval of others and her lack of seeing value in the act of sex overall.

Sex is not a casual event, it's an important action built for the bonding of two special people. Her desire for sexual intimacy with different men instead of valuing herself displays her lack of ability to bond with one man long enough to develop a deep connection. This inability to bond very likely developed in her early childhood and teenage developmental years.

Due to the mental and physical trauma she suffered from, her lack of respect for herself and her own body has lost its importance. Now she's willing to trade her body for a superficial and temporary form of "love" which in reality is the release of the love hormone oxytocin. So the more men she gets a "high" from having sex with the more her body craves sex from a variety of men.

This makes getting this high from one man forever impossible. Her body is used to feeling the touch, the sexual energy, the smell and feeling the penises of different men, one man eventually gets boring. Because having sex with a new man gives her a much higher high than having sex with the same man consistently, she'll always look for a new sexual experience.

The body is a temple and the private parts we possess are called private for a reason. That reason is they are to be shared with someone on a much deeper level than simply pleasure alone. Pleasure alone only releases the love hormone temporarily. But a true bonding experience brings multiple highs without the act of sex.

A mental and emotional bond with a man she's committed to that has been formed over time, will bring her body other highs than just sex. The act of sex is a sacred exchange of energy that has the power to create a new life and that's its true purpose. Its purpose of sex is not solely built for sexual pleasure alone.

The sexual pleasure part of it was created so humans would be encouraged and incentivized to create children because the act of sex is a pleasurable experience. Sex was never meant to be a meaningless act that is taken lightly by a man or a woman misusing it incorrectly to cover up their traumas.

This is the act of abusing sex, and it's also a way of self abuse as a result of low self esteem. Sexual abuse is why sexually transmitted diseases are getting more frequent and more advanced. But these consequences still doesn't deter a promiscuous woman from trading the risk of temporary pleasure for pain and sometimes sterility.

But because of the modern society's promiscuity culture and the sexual innuendos that exist everywhere in the media, the act of sex has lost its true and most sacred purpose and value to women and men. Any woman that exposes her body to such long term consequences for short term pleasure must be avoided at all costs, even sexually.

The Effects Of Sexual Promiscuity Are:

#1. Her Oxytocin Receptors React Less Than A Normal Woman

Oxytocin is a hormone released by the pituitary gland in the brain. This is the same bonding hormone produced when a woman is sexually excited by her partner. And when a woman falls in love or brings a child into the world.

This is why it's called the "Love" hormone. If she has too many repetitive negative experiences in relationships and or too much sexual activity with a variety of men, this oxytocin hormone isn't stimulated and released at the same levels as before.

This creates an untrusting and hardened woman who is burned out hormonally and mentally. A burned out woman has a much harder time bonding with a man than a woman who is not sexually promiscuous and mentally/physically overexposed.

#2. She Has Very Low Levels Of Sexual Discipline

The way that a woman sees her body will determine how many men she's slept with. If a woman doesn't see the value of her body with a positive and healthy perception, then she will sleep with an abundance of different men.

As she gives herself to different men sexually she loses the ability to have sexual discipline because she has become what people call loose. This means that she's easier to sleep with and "loose" with her body due to her lack of sexual discipline.

She doesn't see her body as valuable, and the more she gives it away the less valuable she sees it. So she lives her sexual life on a repetitive cycle of giving her body away for sexual pleasure, while losing more and more self worth in the process.

#3. Impaired Judgement In Picking A Quality Mate

The true purpose of sex is to mate and create a bond that ultimately brings the fruit of their relationship which is children. If a woman is always sleeping with different men then she's surely not taking the time to really get to know these men at deeper levels.

She's likely using her body to try and reel in the attention of a man, while hoping he will take her seriously enough for a relationship. A woman's body and her attractiveness is what she uses to draw in the attention of a worthy mate.

But if she's always sleeping with these men before mentally and emotionally bonding first, she is increasing the odds of these men not taking her seriously enough for a real relationship.

Why? He gets the benefits of sex with her without doing the work it takes to be in a mental and emotional relationship with her. A woman who is easy to have sex with just isn't taken seriously by serious men looking for wives.

#4. An Inability To Achieve An Orgasm

Women keep the men who make her orgasm close because of the natural elusiveness of the female orgasm. A man that can make her orgasm during sex has a much greater chance of keeping her around to have sex with at later times.

That's because he's shown that he can satisfy her sexual needs to climax during sexual intercourse. When a woman has so many different sexual partners it often means that she hasn't found a man that can usually bring her an orgasm during sex.

In reality a woman's inability to orgasm is often a mental obstacle. And if she's looking outside of herself for a man to help her reach an orgasm, then it is very likely that she has a mental block that no man will be able to satisfy.

If a loose woman that finds it hard to orgasm settles with one man in a long term relationship, her inability to orgasm will always become an issue because he's unable to satisfy her sexually.

This will always result in her going outside of the relationship to find a man who can "maybe" bring her to an orgasm. These women are much more likely to cheat all because of her promiscuous past making her sexual discipline very low.

#5. Your Chances Of Being A Cuckold Increases Tenfold

A cuckold by one definition is a man whose wife is sexually unfaithful. So as a result he's often mocked or ridiculed for his sexual inadequacy. But in reality often it's not the mans fault, especially when it comes to a promiscuous woman.

All of the other factors above like her inability to orgasm, her low sexual discipline and her low releases of the oxytocin hormone increases your odds of being humiliated by a woman who blames you for her inability to be sexually satisfied by you.

In reality it's her inability to be satisfied sexually because she isn't in tune with her body anymore. She just doesn't get the same emotional high from sex that she used to. Her promiscuity has numbed her ability to be satisfied by one mans sexual attention.

This pushes her to seek new and more adventurous sexual experiences with men other than you, because you don't make her feel the rush of oxytocin anymore. But she will always find herself on the same cycle with all of the other men she deals with because it's not them, it's her lack of sexual discipline to blame.

#6. Increased Emotional Baggage

A woman who has subjected herself to the different energies of too many men have physical and spiritual residue from all of these male energies that have penetrated her inner fortress. All of these men carry different energies because of their variety of life experiences.

But because sex isn't valuable to her then she doesn't see sex as sacred or an exchange of energy at all. Sex is just something that she does only selfishly for pleasure. And these male energies transfer to her body during sex which she unconsciously and unknowingly picks up, because she doesn't understand her body or sex deep enough.

She doesn't understand the spiritual and energetic consequences of promiscuity. She thinks it's just sex. Sex at its deepest level is a sacred exchange of energy. Not only that, any woman who is highly promiscuous is dealing with an excessive feeling of neediness and inadequacy in her own self and self esteem.

Her over sexualized actions display the deeper unhealed emotions that she deals with mentally. Often drugs, alcohol and other substances can be an additional reason she's promiscuous because these substances are often used to cover up pain.

#7. A Much Higher Chance Of Divorce And Infidelity

Making a promiscuous woman your wife increases your chances of divorce by at least 30%. A woman who has a hard time controlling her sexual urges due to a lack of sexual discipline will find herself in places that push her to cheat like bars and clubs.

Because she has shown that she doesn't have good pair bonding skills, she'll quickly get dissatisfied in a long term relationship when the feelings of love and lust have evaporated within her. Because she's so active sexually, the moment the sex slows down she will look to have those desires fulfilled with another man.

Her promiscuous past will always come to haunt her when she tries to commit to a lasting relationship. Women benefit from a divorce much more than a man does. So that will also come into play when she wants to leave a marriage because her sexual needs aren't being fulfilled. She'll have more of a reason to leave than to stay.

#8. A Desperation For Emotional Validation And Attention

A promiscuous woman is used to using her feminine allure to get the sexual attention of men. This can be incredibly intoxicating to her because of the power she feels over the men who are easily enticed to give her their attention and their lustful desire for her.

This attention not only makes her feel good about herself by feeling wanted, it also gives her temporary sexual satisfaction also. If she's used to having different men want and desire her sexually it's very difficult for her to break that addiction.

Her addiction to male attention will make it extremely hard for her to be satisfied and settled with one mans attention for any long length of time as in a marriage or relationship. She will look to have the men in your circle and her inner circle desire her to give her the high of attention.

This means that she may ruin your relationship with her just to fulfill her own sexual desires. Inevitably she may entice her husbands friends and other men even if not for sex, but for their sexual attention and validation. This will cause issues with your friends and other men that she wants to attract into wanting her sexually while with you.

Throughout history many books have talked about the promiscuous woman. She has been called by many names like the seductress, the succubus, the jezebel, the harlot, Delilah, the man eater, the call girl, the temptress, a ho among so many other titles.

These women have never come to bring peace into the lives of men, they come to bring a man's life chaos, confusion and destruction. That's because internal she's destroyed so externally she destroys her body sexually with promiscuity.

She brings a man these negative energies because her mixing of all of the different male energies into her body, ultimately brings her mental, physical, emotional and spiritual destruction. A man of wisdom knows that he cannot play with fire and expect to not get burned.

But the man who falls for the seduction and sexual temptation that the Jezebel spirit brings, even for just one night will find himself lost to her wicked and destructive ways.

Not only is mixing energies with a promiscuous woman putting your body in danger of std's and death, you're putting your spiritual energy at risk of confusion, bad luck, generational trauma and long term pain.

Stay away from the promiscuous woman and you will give yourself the best chances of finding the worthy wife who will satisfy your needs for loyalty, love, pure sex, spiritual advancement and more importantly life.

Why A Woman Cheats

A woman cheats because in some way with a man she feels deprived. This could mean that she feels deprived of her happiness, her sexual satisfaction, an emotional connection, his time or deprived of an attraction to her man physically.

When she doesn't get enough attention or affection from her man she goes outside of the relationship and finds that attention or affection from another man. This is why any woman who goes out a lot to places like clubs and bars are the women to avoid.

But places like her job, coffee shops, malls and other places outside of the home will provide her with men willing to give her what she lacks. Especially if she's very attractive. When you stop complimenting her and another man compliments her it makes her feel special and desired.

Especially if the affection mental or sexually is lacking in her current relationship. A woman is emotionally vulnerable when her man isn't giving her enough attention, affection and validation. And all it takes is the next man to come into her life and give her what her man at home isn't giving her to get her attention.

A woman is an emotional thinking being. And often her decisions are based upon how it feels in the moment, not on what the consequences of her actions would be later. Because her body will always follow where her emotions take her.

And if her mind isn't being attended to by her current man then another man that gets her attention will eventually get her affection soon after. Once she starts feeling like he will validate her more than you will, and he will give her what you don't, she will draw closer to him and further away from you.

When a woman cheats they are very methodical and think things out much more than a man does. For example, she won't keep the man's number in her phone or she might name the man as a girl. She puts his information in a place you'll never find it. Or she'll cheat with a random man and won't keep access to him.

Most women hide their cheating because they want to keep both of you around because you bring her different things. That's why they'll say things to a man like they don't have a man but they have "friends." In reality these different men bring her things that no one man could never give her for a lifetime.

Because the truth is there's no perfect package of a man in the world. There is no one man that could be everything that she desires and fill her perfectly up with the needs she wants forever. This is only achieved by having multiple men around.

So if you don't fill a woman's needs she will eventually cheat or find an excuse to validate her cheating by saying that you're not giving her what she needs. So always be paying attention to a woman's energy. It will tell you quickly when things are off. This is really your only way to know if she's cheating or her needs aren't getting fulfilled.

Women Always Keep "Other" Men Around

If a woman can deal with you and benefit in some way then she will. It's fun for a woman to deal with multiple men because it validates her attractiveness and satisfies her desire for different male energies. It also validates her ego and boosts her self esteem.

So any man she can talk to and benefit by getting her needs met, of course she'll keep him around as her "friend". And he'll be her "friend" and give her what she wants in the hopes of getting sex from her likely until she starts giving him the cold shoulder. Multiple men gives a woman multiple benefits.

So it's not always about having different sexual partners, it can be about the benefits they give her and the needs they fulfill in her life. These needs can be men who she talks to at night, asks advice about men, has sex with, gives her money, gives her protection, gives her emotional support, men that she's interested in for a relationship or give her rides when she needs it.

There are a variety of reasons why one woman keeps multiple men around. But she keeps these men around because they all have different benefits that serve her wants and her needs. Whatever she lacks in her life, she's looking for a man to fill that hole, even if she knows that it's temporary.

This is why often women who deal with multiple men are often broken women. Most of these men she never sees as marriage material or loves them romantically. In reality she only enjoys what she can get from each of these men physically, monetarily, emotionally and mentally for her benefit alone.

Women are good at making a man feel like he's the only one. Even if she's in a relationship with you she's always looking for better quality men with more to offer than you. Women by nature are wired to always find the best mate, it's called hypergamy.

It's a woman's biological need to look for the strongest, most secure, protective and best suited mate to support her and her child if she has one. So if she wants the benefit of having you around and she's not giving you in return:

-Her life
-Her full attention
-Her full-time
-Her body
-Her presence

Then she's clearly using you for something that benefits her and helps add to her quality of life. When a woman is into a man she wants to spend every moment with him. But if she's hardly available, hard to get in touch with, and you always have to do something for her then she has multiple men around. It's your job to figure out what benefits you serve in her life.

Start by asking yourself:

a. Are you dick on demand?

b. Always around just for a conversation?

c. Useful for rides to work?

d. Just someone to flirt with at work to pass the time?

e. Her trick who gives her money?

f. The man she calls about her problems?

Figure out what need you're filling in her life and then feed her less of it. Then control when she gets it as a reward for good behavior. If she starts acting less interested in you, let her go because she was just using you anyway. She's just mad that you're not giving her what she wants anymore.

A woman with other men floating around her all the time will never give you her full attention. Because she's too busy enjoying getting her needs met by the other men. Plus it boosts her ego and self esteem to feel like she has a lot of men who want to be with her.

A wifely type of woman will only look to entertain the right man with her full attention because she values her time. A woman who scatters her energy around with too many men will never be satisfied with occupying just one man until she gets old.

Her attention span is too short with a man out of habit, so the validation and attention from only one husband will bore her quickly. When her attention isn't valued anymore because she's older and less attractive, then she'll look to find a man to settle with.

Why Women Settle For Weak Men

<u>Reason #1</u>: Loneliness

Insecure, low self esteem and unfocused women settle for lesser men because they're tired of being alone. These women are often unmotivated to do anything outside of work and have a lot of free time. A woman with too much free time will easily fall victim for the social media reward and punishment cycle.

She's constantly seeing others in relationships, which increases her lonely feelings. Because she likely has no highly creative endeavors that would keep her hands busy being productive she resorts to things destructive to her self esteem like social media.

<u>Reason #2</u>: Low Self Esteem

Most women who settle for lesser men feel unworthy of anything special. She doesn't believe that she has what it takes to keep a highly motivated man around because she sees him as better than her.

These women usually have a lot of self destructive habits like overeating, heavy phone usage, alcohol, drugs, etc. Because her self esteem is low, any man that shows her attention can become her man. This sets the bar of her standards low.

<u>Reason #3</u>: She's Lazy

She doesn't want to do the work of finding a great guy. She wants a valuable man but she doesn't see the point in working for it. So she uses social media and dating sites to sort through different men.

A woman has to put her beauty into the world to be seen. But if she refuses to do the work of getting pretty and attractive, she'll attract nothing but low value men.

<u>Reason #4</u>: Her Biological Clock Is Ticking

Her maternal instincts wants to have a child to care for and she needs a baby's father so she finds a willing male donor for her desires.

Any woman who talks about her biological clock ticking is only looking for a man to make a baby with. Once the baby comes, she'll lose interest in him because all she wanted was to answer the call of her biological clock.

<u>Reason #5</u>: She's Lost Hope At Getting Better

She settled for a low quality man because she's disillusioned with men. Her idea of the man she wants doesn't match her reality and she doesn't believe it will ever happen.

Why Women Love Bars And Clubs

Reason #1: For Free Attention

Women are always looking for emotional validation from others to feel good about herself. It doesn't matter if they like the man or woman who's giving them the attention as its attention towards her. Most women have low self esteem and insecurities.

They're used to covering them on the outside with makeup and provocative clothing. But provocative or expensive clothing, hair and makeup don't cover the insecurities inside of her. The club is full of men looking to validate and compliment her so she can forget about her insecurities for the moment.

So it's the perfect place to find lots of male and female validation for any woman. This is why she tries to look as attractive as she can when she goes out. She wants to be attractive enough to attract attention from other men primarily.

Reason #2: Free Drinks

She's almost guaranteed to have guys offer her free drinks if she's attractive enough to get a mans attention. She wants the free drinks knowing she's going to reject 90% of the men she meets.

She also gets the validation of the man who buys her drinks. If she's older or just doesn't feel attractive anymore, bars and clubs serve to make her feel like she still has "it". This is why when a woman ends a relationship her first idea is to go to bars and clubs.

Reason #3: To Have Sex With Someone

Men are always at clubs looking to pick up women because that's the place to go. She knows that most of the men at bars and clubs are looking to have sex and not looking for their future wives.

She just has to dress sexy and be attractive enough to get male attention which isn't hard for most women. Women can get sex much faster than a man can. So bars and clubs are the perfect place to find horny men looking for women to sleep with.

Reason #4: To Find A Man With Money

Men with money can be found in clubs looking to flash themselves as rich men to get a woman's attention. Because they can lure women in by looking like money they can attract women easily at bars and clubs.

And she knows that a drunk man with money is easy prey especially if she's attractive. With the combination of sexual seduction and alcohol it's much easier for her to be forward with a man and to make decisions that are for only one night.

Reason #5: To Get Away From You

There's no other reason to go to a bar or nightclub other than her need for sexual validation. Just to dance isn't a rational excuse when she has to deal with men constantly trying to dance with her.

She's at the club sending out attraction signals and looking attractive to get other men to approach her and validate her self esteem. If she's a married woman she's seeking validation from men outside her husband.

Reason #6: To Re-live Her Wild Younger Days

This means she's trying to relive her younger and more single self. She's trying to rediscover the part of her that's gotten old and boring and looking for excitement. But she'll also be looking to meet old boyfriends from her past which may be at the bars.

Her "old" self is someone she's trying to rediscover because the relationship with you has gotten old, less stimulating and boring. This means that her eyes will naturally be open to new men again also.

A woman who looks at bars and clubs as something to do when she has a man at home is still on the market regardless of what she says. The bars and clubs are places that women go to find validation of the opposite sex.

This means that you don't give her the stimulation or provide her with the free flowing fun that she's looking for. The best bet is to stay away from women, especially older women in their late 30's and 40's who like to drink and go out.

These women are extremely vulnerable to the influences that are only present in the bars and club scenes. This is where her old boyfriends, new possible boyfriends and the negative influences of drugs and alcohol are present.

Any woman who purposely puts herself in the places of temptation isn't a wise woman. And if she hasn't shown that she knows how to have fun without alcohol, bars and clubs then she's limited in her growth and maturity.

This type of woman is extremely dangerous to the stability, quality of life and mental peace of a man because she isn't emotionally mature enough to understand the trap of the bars and clubs. A woman who goes out all the time isn't wife material.

Women And Social Media Addiction

Social media addicts more women than men because men have been raised to have other active hobbies than most women. Social media companies market to women as a whole more than they do men because women are huge internet consumers. Men have sports and video games as alternatives which provides them the mental stimulation and validation that now phones give women.

Women use their phones the same way as men use video games for validation and ranking. The better a man is at sports and video games the higher his score or social ranking is. And the more he feels valued and accomplished, the higher his confidence and self esteem is. This is exactly how social media works for women.

The more often she uses social media by taking pictures of herself and by posting what people like and agree with the more the social media algorithm rewards her self esteem and her feelings of value and accomplishment. Every time she gets a like or a heart on her picture it boosts her self esteem and gives her small hits of dopamine which makes her feel good until "posing & posting" her life becomes normal behaviors.

The dopamine released from the validation and approval she gets, becomes an addiction she craves in order to keep her feeling good about herself. So when she's feeling insecure, she can just dress up, look sexy and take pictures in her room.

The moment that she gets liked and admired on social media and feels the dopamine high from posting, she learns quickly how to work social media in her favor to get more attention and validation. Women love the validation of other women's likes and admires, just like she enjoys a man's validation.

They both still send the same dopamine hormone to her brain that makes her feel good about herself even if for just a moment. The high created from the validation and the approval of other people is a natural and complimentary high for her. Because as a woman she already enjoys getting pretty with clothes and makeup since she was a child.

Over time this easily gained attention and validation becomes an addiction. This is why once she starts posting pictures of herself and getting massive attention from it her posting increases. This hard wires her to become a slave to the high of validation.

The negative result of this social media addiction is that even when she gets into a serious relationship she's still posting her life, herself and her business online. This creates a problem in her relationships, her individual life and in her brain.

Because once she's addicted to social media highs, there is nothing in the world that can replace this high on a regular basis so she constantly seeks it out. This is why you can see two people in the same house or in a restaurant together both on their phones instead of having a bonding conversation or enjoying the moment of them two together.

Not only does it create a desire for a new high constantly in her brain, in her relationships the men on social media will always create the temptation of a new man who's in her dm's or a new man that becomes who she desires over the man she's with.

So girls and women with serious boyfriends in relationships they take seriously shouldn't desire to put provocative pictures on social media. If she wants to be in your inner life she has to accept this fact. But if she's already social media addicted when you met her you've got a problem on your hands.

Start to set up situations that require you both to put your phones up for required amounts of time. When you go out, family time, date night, bed time or when its quality time between you both put the phone down. This is a test to see if she's willing to put you and her time with you over her social media addiction.

If she's not

a. Still looking for a mate
b. Certain that you're the one
c. Unsettled in the relationship

She shouldn't feel the desire to attract sexual attention from other men or anyone else on social media. That's not how a woman who truly desires you will act. If she's obsessed with getting undressed for the camera, you have lost her to the social media algorithm. Things won't get better over time, they'll only get worse.

Why Most Women Act The Same

The modern woman is a product of big business. Especially its marketing department because she's being manipulated, manufactured, controlled and rewarded socially to be who she is. She's watching the trends that other women are "following" behind and then adding them on to herself to imitate.

Now other women will compliment her and "follow" her for being like the rest of the women. She doesn't act different than the rest of the women because she won't be accepted the same as if she was to just cooperate in what's popular. She's now hooked by the social media "reward and punishment cycle".

This set of social media reinforced acceptable behaviors, and beliefs don't exist just online anymore. The approval of her female friends is now determined upon what they see on social media as approved an accepted. So if she wears the popular outfits and live by the standards other women, she's outcasted as different.

So to prevent from being outcasted as different and an individual in her friends group, she now does more and more things popularized by social media to be accepted and validated by her peer group. This results in women of all different ages using the same popular behaviors and saying the same popular things.

Dressing the same, joking the same, gossiping about the same people and ultimately become the same in personality. Studies have repeatedly been found to show that women look at pictures, videos and post pictures of themselves at a much higher rate than men do on social media.

So women are much more vulnerable than men are to get addicted to this reward and punishment feedback loop. As a result of her social media addiction she gets fed a standard of behaviors and beliefs, that most women accept as the way to act. Research has found that 1 in 4 women are on some sort of anti anxiety or anti depression medication.

This is the result of the reward and punishment algorithm used by social media to addict women primarily. The standards of beauty in a women's social media community is aways changing and she can never keep up.

So the result is a lack of self esteem and the need to always keep up with the most beautiful girl standard being set by social media. A woman can't just be herself and be accepted by men or even other women anymore because of social media. She has to get with the program or she believes that she's not good enough.

For Example:

• How many women do you see use the same poses?
• Why do all women wear the same clothes?

- Wear the same hairstyles and hair colors?
- Use the same filters over and over and over?
- Say the same phrases that are popular that year?

Women are doing all of the same things because the social media feedback loop doesn't reward her with likes if she's not "like" everyone else. She doesn't get many likes or rewards on her timeline for being smart and dressing fully clothed.

If she wants the reward from the feedback cycle she has to show a little boob, then turn around and show a little booty and the likes go up. The more skin she shows the more she feels a high from the likes she gets in the reward loop.

For most women, 80% of her behaviors have been primed by the same algorithm as the other women in her social media community. She's posting and taking pictures of things that she knows other women approve of, and also attract male attention.

Because social media has spilled over into her real life she's a slave to social media. When she sees other women behave as online becomes how she wants things to look on the outside. She's lost her individuality and her own personality because she's become like all of the other social media addicted women.

Now she isn't acting her natural feminine self or listening to her own intuition and inner guidance. Her guidance on everything in life has become led by the approval of others and the desire to fit in with all of the other popular women.

Now she's interested in wanting what other women want, instead of her own wants, needs and desires in real life. She's lost her individuality and the connection with her own mind because she's only focused on what the other women think of her. This is how narcissism within her is created.

The more she gets addicted to social media validation, that same desire for validation occurs in the real world. Her whole world is now focused on her looks, her life and how much attention she deserves. That's called narcissism.

Now her thought process has been taught through the repetition of the algorithm to become materialistic, over-sexualized, self focused, self centered. Now she chooses a partner based upon looks over personality. She chooses a man and sometimes a woman who will also be approved by social media.

So she posts pictures of them together and their best moments to make others jealous of the relationship. Now all of her decisions are surface based and never upon what makes her happy, but based upon what makes the algorithm happy.

So the modern woman ends up empty because she never invested positively on developing her own mind more than her body. But she doesn't understand at the time that her beauty will fade over time. And she doesn't understand that the older she gets the less social media validation she'll get.

Because she followed other women on social media instead of following the intuition of her own mind, her social media feed determined her choice of man, her choice of shoes, her favorite tv or movies, favorite makeup, apparel line, etc.

She never truly thought about what made "her" happy because she was too busy following the millions of other women who were also slaves to the social media algorithm until it was too late. Now she's unhappy at 40 years old but stuck in her ways because the program of social media is ingrained in her mind.

Now every free moment she's picking up her phone to check social media because she's addicted and has no other positive hobbies. A woman has to have positive hobbies outside of her phone and social media, or else she will inevitably fall into the hands of the "reward and punishment" feedback loop of social media.

Social media has created generations of women who will always be slaves to that algorithm. Never living their lives truly as themselves. What she thinks is her own thinking but is really just a product of the social media program. This is why so many women are lost, hopeless and unhappy.

The social media algorithm only works if you feed it something. This is why it's called a social media feed. And if she keeps feeding more and more of herself to the algorithm, ultimately over time she'll lose touch with herself, her mind and her own desires. Becoming who the social media program wants her to be.

Dealing With A Woman

"Men Marry Women With The Hope That They Will Never Change. Women Marry Men With The Hope They Will Change. Inevitably They Are Both Disappointed."

-**Albert Einstein**

Choose The Women Who Choose You

Get busy, stay busy and let the woman choose you. Stop wasting your time chasing women, let her chase you. Let her show you her worth and be the one responsible to prove she's worthy of your attention. Don't go out and do all the work by chasing women and over validating her actual value to you other than sex.

When she chooses you, then she has given you the power to lead the relationship. She has given you the value in the relationship because she has to earn your validation instead of you always having to earn hers. Her attraction towards you will keep her interested longer in you than you being the one to earn her attention.

Because women in general have a very short attention span when it comes to men. Especially if she's the prize in the relationship. If she knows that she's the prize, she knows that she has the power to leave whenever she wants to find a better man. This is why you pick a woman who already sees you as the prize in the relationship because she chose you first.

She's already showing that she sees you as valuable. Your job as a man is to become valuable enough that women approach you. Build up your reputation, your character and your bank account in the understanding that a female will find you. Women are hunters and they'll see you and choose. Then treat your dick as exclusive.

Don't give sex to every woman just because you can. This is how you ruin your chances with valuable women who are watching closely but haven't made their move on you yet. Women are always watching, don't forget that! The more exclusive you treat your time, your sex and your presence, the more it becomes like a gift to the women who get to truly experience you.

And the more that other women will want you and your sex due to your exclusivity, because girls talk. Don't focus on the woman you like, focus on the woman that likes you. Why? Because she will be much more likely to follow your lead. Her attraction towards you gives you the power you need to mold her into a team player.

You'll focus on the wrong women if you think with your dick because most men are initially attracted to the sexy, beautiful and attention getting women that all of the other men want also. Sure these women are pretty to have as trophies but not as wives. Outwardly sexy and attractive women know their power to attract a new man other than you.

And a beautiful and attention grabbing woman is much less likely to approach a man they like because she's used to doing the choosing. Highly attractive women have too many male options to choose you and also be submissive to you. You have to always keep your masculine power. And you keep your masculine power by being the one who is getting chased in the relationship.

If she thinks that she's better than you, it's only a matter of time before she finds better than you. Even if her "better than you" is based upon superficial things like looks, money or status. Most beautiful women are materialistic and selfish naturally because she's used to always being the one in the relationship who's worshiped, validated, complimented and admired.

She'll always feel like she's the most important element in the relationship because you'll always have to keep validating her so she stays. When you stop complimenting her, and telling her that she's beautiful she's gone to the next man who will. But a woman who chooses you feels like it's a privilege to get you. So she has a much higher willingness to be loyal in the relationship because in her eyes, he's the prize.

Capture Her Mind And Her Body Follows

Step #1: Build a connection with her mentally before sexually. Because it's hard for a woman to disconnect from a man mentally. But it's much easier for her to disconnect sexually because of promiscuity culture.

How do you develop this connection:

a. Through deep conversation

b. Doing things that develop her trust in you

c. Letting her open up to you emotionally

d. Allowing her to be herself around you

Your job as a man is to give her the best experience she could ever have mentally and physically with any man. This helps you capture her mind and thoughts regardless if she's with you in the future or not.

Step #2: Build a connection with her sexually through love making. Love making is different than normal sex because making love connects to her mind, her body and her soul. Lovemaking is on a different dimension when you understand what it truly is.

Sexually it combines the words you say to her during sex, the way you hold and take control of her body during sex and making sure she orgasms. When you make a woman orgasm her body bonds chemically to you. Use this chemical bond to your advantage by making her climax every time you both have sex.

This means that you have to worry less about you orgasming and more about her climax. A man has a much easier time climaxing because of the way a man's dick is stimulated. Because a woman's pleasure zones to climax are inside of her body, it's on you to find the spots that bring her to a climax.

Letting her sit on top of you and ride is a great way to do this. If you let her use your dick to stimulate her pleasure zones, she can take the charge she needs to find what angles get her closer to a climax. The female orgasm is extremely elusive to even her.

Some women don't climax at all during sex and this means that she won't likely from a man's dick alone. Use her body as a tool to learn what she desires and make sure that she reaches an orgasm during sex and her body is yours.

Step #3: Have deep conversations where you let her talk and reveal all of her secrets to you. By being open and listening to her you'll become a safe place for her thoughts, her beliefs and more importantly her desires. Once you understand her wants and desires you've entered her inner life.

Let her reveal to you the woman most people will never get to see. You can't seem like you're judging her. Be her non judgement zone and she'll tell you all of her secrets. Once she feels comfortable telling you everything, then you've penetrated the inner thought life of her mind.

And now you can use what you know about her desires and her inner thoughts to your advantage. Possess her mind and you will automatically take hold of her body. Her mind is her main computer and holds all of her hidden secrets that she keeps away from the outside world.

Learn her inner most thoughts and her mental, emotional and sexual desires and you'll know everything about her. A person can only speak what they think in their minds. You don't have to be a mind reader, just listen to her tell you what's on her mind to know.

Step #4: Bring something new to her life. This makes her look at you like a hero that's trustworthy and reliable. This means teach her new information, a new outlook on life, a new hobby or take her on a new experience.

When you teach a woman something new she gains a respect for you that translates into mental and physical attraction. Now when she tells others about what you've taught her, or goes to the places you first took her to, she'll think of you.

Women want a man who can teach and lead her to new things. Not a man who she has to be the teacher and leader of because that's boring to her. When a woman has to teach a man she sees him as her son, instead of a man she wants to have sex with.

If she learns new things from you it makes her feel like your daughter and you her father. All women crave the teachings and protections of their father especially if she never had a father present in her life consistently and desired one.

Her attraction to you will fade if you don't teach her anything new because she has to appreciate your mind to value it. Your mind is what sets you apart as a man from more attractive and wealthier men than you. She has to respect your opinions and your beliefs on everything she does.

This means that she has to respect your mind and your thoughts enough to want to listen to your thoughts and ideas. If she doesn't want to listen to you willingly, then she sees you as weak and beneath her. This means that you don't have a hold of her mind and over time you will lose your connection to her body.

If you capture her mind and automatically her body follows. If you follow these steps and take your time to know who she really is in her mind, you now have the upper hand and the keys you need to stay in control of the relationship.

Listen To And Learn Her Desires

A woman's desires are what lead her life choices, behaviors and attitude in life. Women who desire material things can be rewarded with these things she desires to keep her attention. But remember that material things are only temporary highs.

Women who desire less physical materials desire more emotional desires. Rewarding her emotional desires for her good behaviors are an easy way to keep her attention. Fulfilling a woman's emotional desires last longer than rewarding her material desires.

That's because a woman's happiness by nature is built upon emotional pleasure. Pay attention to what kind of woman she is. Is she emotionally motivated or is she materially motivated? Does she desire physical touch, talk and walks or new purses, random gifts and surprise dinner and dates?

Even if she likes material things it's emotionally driven at its core because it makes her feel wanted and desired by the man she's with. But listen to her and look at her lifestyle. What emotion is her desires driven by? The desire for more material things, emotional things or is she driven by the simple things in life?

Understand her basic desires because that will show you what she needs to be rewarded with. Understanding her basic desires also tells you if she desires something you don't have or don't have much of like time or money. If you don't have enough money she'll leave you for a man with more money.

If you don't have enough time for her she'll find a man who does have the time for her. Your awareness of her desires helps you understand what she believes will make her happy even for the moment. That means if what she desires pull strong enough on her, she'll fill those desires even if it means hurting you in the process.

For example if she has a strong enough desire for negative obsessions like sex, money or drugs you will always lose her to those desires in the long run guaranteed. If her desires are to obtain money, fame, status, looks and the validation of others you will lose her to those desires also.

Her desires will always pull and tug on her mind until they're fulfilled. This is why a man who gives a woman everything he can give her but what she truly desires, loses her to a man who fulfills her desires. This is the reason why so many good men get cheated on.

She may desire a good man emotionally but a bad guy sexually. Your only job is to learn and know her desires from the beginning. Understanding her motivations and desires helps you stay ahead of her in the game when her desires present themselves around you both.

And when you need her to feel motivated, appreciated and rewarded, by understanding her desires you have an advantage over most men in relationships. Most men don't know how to motivate their woman with her desires when she needs it.

They never take the time to focus on anything but their own desires for sex, so they lose their women to other men who can fulfill her mental and or emotional desires. Trigger her desires for your own advantage by rewarding her with her desires.

This is all social media has done with the reward and consequence cycle. They reward women with their emotional desires of acceptance, validation and approval. Because of their understanding of a woman's desires, social media platforms are now billion dollar companies.

Use the same winning formula that they use by liking what she does right and not rewarding behaviors you don't like. Motivate her by rewarding her good behaviors with the desires of her heart. Reward her for her great work, loyalty and for proper behaviors just like women do men with leveraging sex.

We all need to feel rewarded anytime we're doing something consistently or we'll lose our motivation to act. She needs a reward so she has a clear reason in her mind why she's with you. It's your job to make her staying with you rewarding. The key is to only reward her for good behavior.

Don't just randomly reward her with something that she didn't earn. If you just reward her randomly your rewards will lose its value and its strength over time. Only reward her for doing something that you asked her to do, and any other actions that you want to keep encouraging your woman to do.

When you do this she starts to see and feel that giving to you is rewarding her life in some way. This is called positive reinforcement. You're rewarding a good behavior to motivate the person to keep doing it. This is actively using the reward response in a persons brain to keep them wanting to do things for you.

If you don't motivate and reward a woman with her desires to stay with you, then another man will reward her with her desires to leave you. Give her something to work for in the relationship to keep her mind focused and engaged on you.

Her Respect Weighs More Than Her Love

All love feelings fade over time naturally. But when she respects you she'll come back years later to see about you. That's because love feelings are replaceable but respect takes longer to fade. Her respect can turn back to attraction, but her love alone cannot turn back into respect.

Once a woman doesn't respect you, it's incredibly hard to make her desire to trust and respect you again. You always want a woman to respect you more than she loves you. She is even much less likely to cheat on a man that she respects, versus a man that she only loves but doesn't respect.

When she stops respecting you as a man, she'll start exploring her options to find other men she looks up to and respects. This is why so many women leave relationships because they have lost respect for the men they're with. Men get comfortable with their woman and then allow her to use the word love to manipulate them into doing things that lose her respect.

All because they don't understand that if she doesn't respect you, she can't truly love you. You must always keep her respect by standing up for yourself and your opinions during your conflicts with her. And never compromise your desires for her desires just to make her happy, because you'll lose her respect in the process.

When a woman feels like she loves you more than she respects you her emotions are in control, not her logic. You want her to love you deeper than her emotions. You want her to love you with her logic. When she loves you with her logic, she'll love you with her mind and not just her body. That's because emotions are irrational and can change at any moment, logic doesn't.

This means that when it comes to her making decisions about the quality of the relationship, she'll base that decision on solid facts and not always changing feelings.

In this day and age the idea of love doesn't mean much. A woman can say that she loves you, but isn't in love with you. In reality all this means is that she cares for you, but doesn't respect the man that you are.

This means that she doesn't really love you because she doesn't know what love truly is. Logical love is understanding, patient and unconditional. But emotional love is fickle, selfish and based upon feelings not facts. Most women base the idea of love on emotions, feelings and specific actions.

You won't change the way a woman loves, so add her respect with her love so she loves you with her emotions and her logic. In this way you capture her whole mind, not just a small part of it. A woman who respects you even if she leaves won't make it a difficult process. Her respect for you will have her checking up on you later in life when you're not together.

But a woman who doesn't respect you will do things like sleep with other men in your bed, talk to other men while you're together and do things to hurt you on purpose. A woman's respect for you weighs much more than her love for you. As a man always remember that a woman's love is emotional, situational and conditional, but her respect is logical, solid and intentional.

The Key: Your respect taps into her logical mind and it will stay there forever as long as you don't do things to be disrespectful to her.

Speak Up For Yourself To Be Respected

Always speak your mind and never suppress your truth when dealing with any woman. This is how a man keeps and maintains his respect in the eyes of his woman and the other women in his life. Most guys are afraid of saying how they truly feel because they're scared to hurt a woman's feelings, but it's bigger than that.

Speaking up for yourself takes courage and a woman admires a courageous man because she can't walk all over him. No woman will never respect a man that she can walk all over. Even if she gets upset from you standing your ground and sticking up for yourself ultimately she has to respect it. Expect her to get upset but she'll eventually come to her senses.

She needs your honesty to develop a true respect for you. If you go with everything she suggests and wants then you will ultimately be loved but not respected. And remember that respect weighs much more than love.

Your unapologetic honesty shows her that you won't just say whatever she wants just to please her because you need and want her approval of you.

In any type of relationship the one who needs the approval of the other is in the submissive role. A woman will never develop trust in a man who is submissive and always looking for her approval. Because internally a woman understands that you will say whatever you need to say just to make her happy, even lie.

A woman can't be submissive and feel safe with a man that's too afraid to lead the way with the truth. Regardless if it hurts her or not. A woman can feel if you don't really agree but you're just going along to get along. Agreeing to everything kills her attraction to you because it's your opposing masculinity that she craves and desires sexually.

This opposition of masculine energy is why women fall for bad boys. Most bad boys will say how they feel, while good guys say whatever they think doesn't hurt her feelings. A woman gets bored if it's only her way all the time. She wants to see if you have your own opinions and beliefs. Because when a man states his own opinions, it shows her that he is decisive in his choices.

This says to a woman that you know who you are. By you being honest she'll gain respect for you because you won't compromise yourself for her. She sees that unlike other guys you won't compromise your ideas and your beliefs to her pussy power. Ultimately, a woman is built to challenge you as a man for the leadership role in the relationship.

This is the natural order of a man and a woman. She will always challenge your strength as a leader. So if you won't compromise your truth just to make her happy she'll accept and respect your leadership willingly. She'll then fall into her place as the submissive role. Holding in how you really feel is like taking poison every time you do it.

Because it will always come back to hurt you in the end emotionally in the form of resentment and the loss of your confidence. It also hurts the dynamics of the relationship because she'll see you as weak. This will lead her to look outside of the relationship eventually for a man that challenges her. So always speak your mind.

Show her that she can't push you around, make you submissive or dangle sex in front of your face to get her way. As a man never let her get you to compromise yourself ever. When you say your truth don't be emotional, purposely hurtful and harsh, be a man about it. Always stay calm, cool and collected when you respond to her.

Look her straight in the eyes and say your truth firmly and confidently. Never get emotional, extremely upset and over react in your conversations with her. If you do you'll lose respect because she'll know you can't handle your own emotions. If she sees that she can make you emotional, then she'll purposely do things that will pull you out of character.

You can never win any conversation with a woman by becoming emotional with her. She's very comfortable fighting emotionally. So stay logical, firm in your opinions and don't let insults, her anger or her outbursts pull you into her emotions. You can never keep a woman's respect if she sees that she can pull you into emotional fights. A King is always on the throne.

That means regardless of how much she disagrees with your opinions or tries to get under your skin stay calm and cool. A man always says what he means and means what he says. This means that you can never be afraid to stand up for your ideas and opinions. If you stand tall on your morals and opinions as a man regardless of how she reacts then you will always keep her respect in tact.

Let Her Invest Time & Money Into You

The more time and money she spends on you, the more attached she will be in the long run. That's because she's made a time and emotional investment in you. The more time, emotions and money that a woman invests in you, the less likely she'll leave that investment quickly. This is the opposite of how most men play the game.

Normally a man does all of the investing in her then he gets attached while she isn't. He spends all of his time and money trying to wine and dine her to show her that he's worth her time. But inevitably all he's doing is showing her that she's the valuable one in the relationship. Because a valuable person isn't trying to convince the other person of their value.

They know their value and require others to invest in them. You're the valuable one and if you want her to see you that way then you let her invest in you first. Let her spend her money, let her do the most of the phone calling and making the effort to find time to spend with you. Let her invest in you.

If you let her do the majority of the investing then she'll be hesitant to take a loss on her investment in you. Let her do the work to earn her role in your life, not the other way around. Let her make time to spend with you so that her time investment is high. A woman will value her time invested in you more than her financial investment in you.

So make her put in as much time investment as possible. She'll be hesitant to give up quickly on you because she doesn't want to invest that much time and money in you and get nothing for it. If you don't keep her investment in you high she will intentionally do just enough to get you attached to her then ease up.

This is how she gets you and so many other men attached in the beginning thinking that she's wifey. All she did was let you make all of the time, money and emotional investments into her. She just played the good girl role to keep you investing in her until you were hooked. Then later once you both got serious in the relationship she switched up on you.

Let her do all of the investing because she will at first. Because in most cases a woman will always put her best foot forward on the gas pedal when she meets you because her feelings are involved. But once she's gotten comfortable and her logic kicks in then she'll ease up on the gas pedal to see if you'll give back.

So selfishly when she invests in you, she's looking to get back at least what she spent on you. This is why you make her invest her time and do 80% of the effort in everything. This sets the standard for the relationship because she sees that you're the valuable one to be invested in, not just her like she's used to with most men.

Make her earn your pleasure and your company instead of you trying to earn hers. If you do this when dealing with a woman you'll get both. A man has to use the same game a woman uses on her to win. If you use her own game against her then she won't see it coming from a mile away. Women aren't used to men dealing with her using strategy and thought.

This is because most men are dealing with her through lust and desire. Let her invest in you and you'll reap the rewards. Remember that value doesn't market itself because it's valuable and not everyone can afford it. Make her invest in your value and she'll value you, your time and your energy. If not let her go for one who will.

Your Attention Can't Be Free

Make your woman work for your:

1. Conversation
2. Time
3. Texts
4. Affection
5. Sexual Energy

Your time, energy and attention has to come with a price. If it's free eventually you'll be used up until you're left with nothing. Nobody values long term anything free and Un earned especially a woman. Only reward a woman when she invests in you because women get free attention from lonely men all the time.

If you give her free attention like the other men what makes you any different? Only give her good morning and other sweet texts when she's following your requirements to keep your attention. If she isn't following the requirements to keep your attention, she gets no free attention from you period.

This teaches her if she wants the extras from you she has to earn it. You're the value in the relationship and she has to earn access to that value. But this means that you can't be a low quality man also. If you're a low quality man then this won't work. Your attention has to be treated like it's valuable, special, rare and hard for just anyone to get access to.

Because if you don't make her earn your attention she won't value it because it's free and too easily accessible. This means she'll look at your time and attention as nearly worthless. If she can get your attention whenever she wants to it holds no value as a reward to her. But she will look at another mans attention as valuable who treats his time and attention that way.

This is why you never give her the attention and validation she doesn't earn. No compliments, gifts or extra ordinary treatment if she doesn't earn it because she won't value it over time. Giving her access to all of your approval and attention all of the time, whenever she wants it is how you create a spoiled and entitled woman who thinks she deserves more than she does.

If you give her all access to your attention and validation then her efforts to keep you around will fade over time. That's because anything a person doesn't have to work for makes room for laziness and familiarity. Then once she gets bored with your free attention she'll start looking for other mens attention.

Your attention is all you have to offer her mentally. And if you don't see your attention as valuable she won't either. Women need a man's validation to feel confident. For example if she goes out into the public and no men look at her she feels unattractive, unwanted and her self esteem suffers.

Little validation and attention given freely to a woman means that she'll work harder to gain that validation from you. And once she gets the validation and attention from you she'll value it because she had to work for it. Don't over validate her with a bunch of compliments like other men.

Because a man that over validates and compliments her is not what she desires to be in a long term relationship with. These men are located all over social media and easy to find for her. Only deal with a woman willing to put in the work. If she doesn't want to earn your attention then shake her for someone who will.

Value what you have to give a woman and always make her invest in you more than you invest in her. Making her work is less about her and more about you retaining your value in her eyes. This means that you must place real value on what you have to offer, for her to value you and what you have to give. It always has to be at least an equal exchange of value between you and her.

It must be an equal exchange of energy when dealing with any woman and not just a one way exchange to keep her respect and admiration. By giving a woman access to your value in the forms of your time, your validation and attention you're returning that value based upon what she gives you to earn it.

Giving a woman for free what she doesn't earn is a formula for creating a spoiled and entitled woman that will eventually take you for granted. Not even your sex should be free because it's an equal exchange of energy between two people. Nobody deserves anything for free, they get rewarded for what they work for. And when dealing with a woman it should be no different.

Make Her Earn Your Sex

If her pussy is a prize to you then your dick is the prize to her, don't forget that. Don't let her make you believe that her pussy is the prize just like all of the men she's been with before you. She wants your dick just as much as you want her pussy don't get played. In many ways your dick is more powerful than her pussy.

Because if you use your dick game right then your dick game can break her down, make her submissive to you and your dick game can also build her back up. Women worship dick, they've just allowed society and culture to make you believe that her pussy is more valuable than your penis.

Women worship a man who has great sex and understands how to use his sex to his advantage. You can use her desire of your dick to build up her attraction to you. So that means that you can't give it to her every time she wants it. You have to leverage your dick as a reward for her good behaviors, just like she leverages your access to her pussy.

This works to get your way with a woman because she's used to always getting her way by flaunting the illusion of pussy in front of weak men. She knows how to use her pussy to get her way, so you better learn how to use your dick the same way. Women don't know what to do if a man isn't influenced by the thought of her pussy to give her, her way.

She's so used to dealing with weak minded men who don't understand the power they also hold between their legs. But when she meets a man who can control his sexual urges enough to not be manipulated by his desire, it drives her crazy from the rejection she feels. But men are always dealing with this form of sexual rejection.

She's not used to being rejected from sex. For most women that never happens. When she wants sex from a man 99% of the time she gets it. This is why you have to switch the game up on her and play the game she plays with men against her.

This is how you beat a woman at her own game. You don't react the way she expects you to and it drives her crazy. So understand that rejecting her of dick is going to make her angry. But you tell her that she has to earn it and if she wants it she will!

Make her earn your dick by:

- Cooking your favorite food
- Wearing that dress/lingerie you like
- Listening to what you say
- Behaving the right way
- Doing the things that you like

She has to do things to earn your dick, not the other way around if you want her to value it. Once you understand the power of attraction and how powerful your dick is to her life, you'll stop getting manipulated by your desire for pussy. A woman understands the power of using her sexual attraction, but most men don't.

She uses her pussy to get free drinks, money, free attention and whatever else she wants from men. She won't respect you if you allow her to do the same to you. She controls her pussy output. And if she can manipulate you sexually like the other men, then what makes you any different than the rest of those weak men? Nothing!

She can only manipulate a man who believes that her pussy is more important than what he has to offer. Because while he's trying to earn her pussy she's getting whatever she wants from him. This is how a gold digger gets her way by manipulating a man's desire for pussy.

They buy her things, take her out, spend their time, money and energy on her and often these men still get no pussy in the end from her. Just the illusion of the pussy was enough to get him to give up his valuable time and money.

She just sold these men an imaginary fantasy that she manipulated and turned into physical possessions all because she valued and controlled her sexual energy. When you don't value and control your sexual energy she knows that you don't value your dick. Now she can easily run game on you.

Use the same game on women by never giving her your sex when you first meet her. This will set you apart from 99% of men who can't control their lust to bust. It allows her to build up sexual energy and the desire for your sex. Now she looks forward to getting your sex from you because you switched up the game on her.

Now you're in the position of power instead of her. She will crave sex from you and try to set up situations where she can get it from you. But to get it she has to earn your sex. Now like the gold digger she has to do what you want her to do just to get access to your dick.

Now like a man would normally be, she's living in her mind and intensifying the illusion of how sex with you would feel. This will intensify her orgasm also when that time comes. Because the longer you have a woman living in her head and fantasizing about you the better it will always work in your favor.

You want a woman to live in her fantasies about you. You want her sitting at home thinking about why you haven't given it to her. And how it would feel once she does get it from you. This is dick mastery only for the men who know the value their dick has in her life.

This simple step alone will increase her curiosity, attraction and desire for you if she has to wait. You'll also change the normal routines she's used to with men. This will automatically make her think that you're different which is what you want.

Use this technique with a woman that you really like and she will bond to you easier. Dick discipline is the most powerful technique a man can use on a woman. Once you understand the power of your dick you now can use it to manipulate and reward her behaviors instead of her rewarding and manipulating yours.

Women Don't Value What Comes Easy

What motivation does she have to be happy when you've given her access to everything in your life? She doesn't, because you present no challenge or mystery to her anymore. This leaves no room for surprises or variety which women need to be emotionally stimulated or in her words "happy" in the relationship.

A woman needs variety in a relationship or she gets bored quickly. The man that gives her the most emotional stimulation she stays with, even if it's negative emotional stimulation. This is why so many women stay in bad relationships because the "bad" guy gives her someone to "feel" with.

If she can't "feel" happy she'll take feeling mad, sad, angry and anxious in a bad relationship. This is just how the brain of a woman is wired. This is why women gossip about each other, stay on their phones and watch toxic reality tv shows in such abundance.

Once she gets settled in the relationship she gets bored because she doesn't have to fight for anything anymore. She doesn't have to earn your attention or compete with the thought of you leaving her like she did in the beginning of the relationship. Eventually her lack of excitement when dealing with you, turns to a lack of attraction towards you.

This is why she then starts to limit the sexual contact. Her attraction levels to you have been diminished to low levels because you give her everything too easy. A woman wants to feel like she has to earn your attention. In a marriage or long term relationship with you, there's nothing to earn anymore because most men stop striving to become their best selves.

She stops fearing losing him because he's stuck. They given all of their attention towards making her happy, and even compromised their true feelings just to give her what she wants. But this always backfires on the man she's with. Because over time she doesn't value what he has to give anymore even if it's a lot.

It's human nature to lose our sense of value towards anything that is given often and freely. If she has all of the access to your bank account, your time, your attention and your sex what does she have to work for anymore? What's left for her to prove? What's left to earn? What reason does she have to treat you special or appreciate your I love you's?

There's nothing left for her to earn because she's already won the prize of getting access to everything that you have. Boring! Once she doesn't have to fight for her starting spot on the team, she starts believing that she deserves to be on the team and in that starting role. This starts the process of her feeling entitled to that position, so she stops working hard to keep that starting spot.

To stay happy a woman in a relationship has to feel like she's earned a valuable position as your woman or wife.

You have to keep a woman on her toes by not giving up too easily your validation and your attention. Make her earn it! She has to value your time more than physical possessions to stay happy long term.

Because even the high of her getting money and gifts from you doesn't last forever. She has to be afraid of losing you, because losing your attention and your time would be losing the best thing to ever happen to her life. This means that you have to always be changing for the better and getting more interesting by learning new things.

If you're stuck in life you'll become boring and she'll become curious about other men. So always work to become your best self through growth so her attention will be on all of the other women looking at you instead. A happy wife or woman in general is a woman who feels like she has to work to stay in your life.

That's because she'll always feel accomplished when she earns the reward of your time, your money and your attention when she gets it. Most men in long term relationships don't make women fight to be in their lives. They're always too available for her demands.

And they're too quick to submit to her every want and need without requiring her to do the work to earn anything. These men find out the hard way that spoiling any woman does the opposite of keeping her happy. It ultimately only creates a spoiled and entitled woman who expects to be given everything without giving anything of value back in return.

This is what creates a miserable and one sided relationship. If the happy wife happy life motto was so perfect then why are so many women who are given everything in relationships unhappy? Because they're bored and have nothing to work for anymore in the relationship.

Any woman who gets everything without doing any work to earn it will become spoiled and entitled naturally. For example, give everything to a child without requiring them to give anything back in return and how do they act? Spoiled, entitled and manipulative. This is basic human psychology.

We feel like we deserve what we're given frequently and freely. And when we don't get it anymore we get upset and throw an adult temper tantrum which is anger and manipulation. Anything we're given too much of just isn't appreciated. And a woman won't value what she's given too much of freely without any effort on her end.

So if you're giving your woman all of your attention, your sex, your money, gifts, compliments and full access to your attention at any time she wants it, then you're spoiling her. You're teaching her that she can have whatever she wants from you without requiring her to earn and value what she gets access to in your life.

This is why later in the relationship she starts feeling bored and "unhappy". This is when she starts going out with her friends more often, and she starts limiting your access to sex to only times when you earn it. This is because women already know the game, but it's men that don't understand it at all.

Never give a woman what she doesn't earn if you want her to stay mentally engaged in a long term relationship. For example you only give a woman a bigger position like your "wife" if she's earned it. You don't just give her the position of your wife because she's pretty, nice to you, has a great body or has good sex. That's only you seeing what you're going to get from her.

What is she getting out of the deal with you that will keep her focused on you? What she's getting out of the deal is access to your money, resources, validation and attention, but only if she earns it. These are your only bargaining chips of value. Anything that she doesn't have to earn from you will always be taken for granted over time, regardless of how much you value it.

Never give her more time, money or energy than she's earned because why would she value anything you gave her too easily? This means that you have to understand the power of telling her "no" sometimes in the relationship. She won't have a problem telling you no, so why would you? No is a healthy part of a relationship because it establishes boundaries.

You have to stop giving her random gifts of your time, money, validation and attention if she doesn't earn it with good behavior, willing sex and a positive attitude. If not it's time to let go and move on quickly. Reward her and she'll stay, don't she'll get spoiled. It's really that simple. We value what we earn and we don't value what comes too easily, especially a woman.

She Sees Marriage As A Business Deal

Why would any man sign a contract that a woman has an incentive to break? It works in her favor to have you sign a marriage contract and then break the contract with divorce papers because she gets half of everything you've worked for. The more a man makes the less likely a woman will divorce him.

This says to a smart man that for a woman marriage is about being with a man who symbolizes as a profitable business. Marriage for her is a profitable business where she gets the benefit of a higher salary the richer a man is. For example, would you risk a high salary and high paying job for a low paying job? No! So why would you expect her to.

The more you have the more she benefits by being married to you. And the more you have the more she benefits from divorcing you. So either way she wins the business transaction by marrying you. Relationships of high earning men over $150,000 dollars a year in average income states are 20% less likely to divorce.

This is versus an average of a 45% divorce rate among middle class and low income earners. Love is not the foundation of a relationship or a marriage like most people believe. You can build a solid marriage foundation based upon feelings that will always change.

Marriage and relationships have to be built upon solid principles. And it's these solid principles that provide each person in the marriage with strict rules, guidelines, procedures, morals, values and specific actions that allows each partner to know if they're violating the relationship or not.

This is just like building any successful business. For a business to be successful it must have rules and procedures that each employee must follow or their job will be instantly terminated. The business is justified in terminating that employee's job contract because the employee knowingly broke the rules.

They understood that those specific actions were clear breaches of the employment contract. Just like if you're in a marriage with a woman and she knowingly does things in the relationship that symbolize disloyalty to the relationship. By her doing these specific actions she is agreeing to terminate the marriage contract.

This is how marriages have to be seen by a man and a woman. Marriage must be seen and treated as a business because it gives each other the ability to know clearly the expectations that each person has for the marriage to be successful.

Too often in marriages one or both partners knowingly do something to violate the marriage and expect for the marriage to be successful after their breach of marriage expectations. They don't understand why one of the partners have mentally left the relationship after their discretion.

But once the rules, guidelines and trust in the relationship is broken the marriage greatly loses its ability to stand the test of time. Before you're legally married by the state you must sign a marriage contract, just like if you were doing any other form of business dealings.

A contract is starting a legal union together called marriage between two different people aka companies. Why else would there be a contract you both gave to sign if marriage were not recognized by the government as a business? It's the people in it who have been led to believe that somehow it's the feelings that determine the contract.

The feelings are what compelled both parties to pursue and sign the contract, but not what bind the contract. It's the signature and rules stated on the contract that solidify the agreement. And those rules are specific actions which are beyond feelings. This is why feelings don't constitute a marriage. Specific roles, guidelines and duties are what truly constitute a marriage.

It is the actions and duties that make people feel like they want to stay married. These two ideas have to be separated and clearly understood before you as a man allow yourself to get pulled into the idea of marriage. She has to act and behave like a wife way before she is even eligible of the act of signing a marriage contract.

Even in the marriage contract there has to be certain rules and set guidelines that each party is held to. And these set actions includes consequences if one or both people breach that marriage contract. That would make you and your spouse think twice before you make any decisions that you both knowingly understood would violate the terms of the marriage contract.

This gives you both as partners in the marriage business a clear direction and a clear set of actions to follow in the marriage. This protects you as a man much more than it protects her who will benefit regardless if she divorces you or not.

For example: If she cheated on you or took money out of your accounts without disclosure to you, then she is knowingly violating the business agreement of the marriage. Without clear consequences in the marriage it is doomed from the start.

This is why you must protect yourself, your money, your growth and all of the time you've put in to build a life for yourself. As a man who will already get the bad end of the business deal if you're not careful, by treating and seeing any marriage to a woman as a business agreement and business arrangement you're now prepared for the business deal. She already is!

Before You Move In With Her Understand...

1. She Stops Fearing Her Female Competition

Now she doesn't think that she has to work as hard to keep you anymore. This will result in her not only taking your presence for granted, but it will result in her taking her need to keep herself up for you for granted. This is why so many women begin to let themselves go once a man moves in with her.

She knows that she doesn't have to compete as hard with other females to keep you anymore, because she's done the work she needs to get you close enough to watch you. So she stops trying to compete with other women outside of the relationship for your attention because she's already won the prize of your presence everyday and your primary attention.

Because she sees you every day she loses her competition anxiety that she had when you're not living with her. When you weren't living with her she had to wonder what you have going on when she's not around. Because she didn't know all of the time what you're up to, it created an anxiety that you might be doing something she doesn't want you to do.

She fears you're doing things like cheating, hanging with your friends around other girls, on social media talking to other girls, etc. Women watch closely the men they're in relationships with who aren't around them 24/7 very closely, even if you know that or not. As soon as she starts to like you she starts monitoring everything that she can see for other female attention.

This means that she's watching who likes your social media posts, seeing who comments, monitoring your time spent on there, your outside whereabouts, when you're at home and when you're at work. That's why she randomly texts you and calls you at work and other times of the day.

It's not just because she likes you, she's watching you. She's trying to secure your attention and see where else your attention is going so she can focus it only on her. So once she moves in with you or you move in with her she knows that she can relax more because all she has to do now is monitor your social media and your phone calls.

She already has the majority of your time. As long as she doesn't have you living with her she will always have competition anxiety. So she'll always try to keep her looks, her attitude and her attitudes in check. But once you move in together there's no incentive to keep these things up.

2. She'll Use Constant Criticism To Get You To Change

This is technically called beta-tization through 1000 concessions or simply called nagging you into submission. This doesn't happen when you're dating because she's much less likely to criticize you because she doesn't want to run you off.

But once you move in with her she will try and get you to submit to her way of doing things with an array of suggestions about how you should do things now that you're both together. They'll start with small things like where you should keep your toothbrush or how you're supposed to wash the dishes and where exactly they go.

And then with bigger things like what time she wants you to go to sleep or when "she" wants to have sex. All of these "suggestions" of how she wants you to do things are her way of taming you to be submissive to the ways she thinks you should act and behave. She does this because it makes her feel more in control of you and the relationship for her own security.

Each time you submit to these little requests you become less and less interesting to her because you are being totally under her behavioral control and submission. When you weren't living together she couldn't control how you lived your life.

If you let her dictate how you live your life now, in her eyes you'll become less of a challenge and more boring and beta in her eyes. This is why it's much better for you both to have your own places to live even when things get serious.

3. She'll Feel Like She's In Control Of The Rules

When you move into another person's house you are now subjected to their rules. They have the authority to tell you how things are going to be done because they are the major responsibility holder of the residence. If you don't follow her rules you will always be under the threat of being kicked out.

If you're not doing what she wants you to do, and how she wants you to do it then you will have to face her negativity until you do it her way. That negativity will come in the forms of attitudes, nagging and aggressive behaviors towards you because you're not acting how she wants you to act under her roof.

If you're both going to move in together then its much better if she's moving into your place and not the other way around because you have the authority. It doesn't matter how nice she is or how well things start in the beginning, there will always come a time where she wants you to do something bad enough that she'll tell you to do it or get out of "her" house.

She will always enforce her boundaries with the threat of you getting out when you live with her. This is without question. If you move in with her it has to be on your terms. But this is difficult to achieve because ultimately she does have the most leverage.

A woman will always be happier in her own environment where she controls the environment. For example, next time you see boys and girls playing together pay attention to how the girls tell the boys what to do. That's her nature since a child.

4. You Could End Up Homeless

If you as a man have to live with a woman and you don't have your own place or the ability to get and maintain your own place you're setting yourself up for disaster. That's because at anytime she can get mad and make you get out of her house lawfully.

It doesn't matter how much you've contributed to the rent or how much furniture you've bought, by law you have to get out of her house. Not having your name on the lease will always by law put her in the ultimate position of authority over you.

She will let you pay the bills, buy the food, buy things for the kids if she has them and do everything like you own the place also but in reality you don't. This will always be in the back of her mind that she holds this power over you.

And once she gets fed up with you, she still gets to benefit from all that you've done to contribute to her quality of living and you'll get nothing for it in the long run. And if she controls the rental lease or the property by it being in her name she'll also feel a sense of power over you.

This over time pushes her to lose respect for you because she knows that she can ruin your stability at any time. No woman will ever stay respectful or look up to a man that she is in any way responsible for his basic needs. She can't see you as a man because depending on a woman puts you in the position of being a child.

Once she begins to see you as a child because she's taking care of your basic needs, she'll no longer see you as attractive sexually so the frequency of sex will diminish along with her respect in conversation. You must always be in full control of your own living environment financially.

And never let your basic needs like shelter be controlled by a woman. Even if you move in with her keep yourself a stash of money just in case things go bad just to keep yourself from ending up homeless. You as a man have to always put yourself in the position of ownership and stability, not ever allowing yourself to be fully reliant on her.

She Can Leave You At Any Moment

You never know what tomorrow will bring, so always be prepared mentally and financially for her leaving you. And if she leaves you, let her go. When its over, its over! Don't make yourself look bad or compromise your manhood by begging and pleading for her to stay with you.

She's already been mentally done with you so get your emotions in check and move on to the next stage of your life. She'll come looking for you in the future if she respects you still. And you'll have your chance to make her feel like she made you feel if you act like a man when she leaves. But you have to uphold yourself up as a man to be respected.

This means that you can never beg her to stay with you ever! You'll ruin any chance of her respecting you when you do this. She'll see you as weak versus if you just move on she'll see you as strong. If you beg her to stay and act overly emotional by getting angry, upset, vengeful or sad, she will be sure to drag your reputation and your business into the street just to hurt you more.

Things and people change. So don't be mad about it, just think of all of the fun you had and then how she tried to hurt you by doing you bad so you can see the bigger picture. Everything changes, even relationships and the levels of love, her level of love for you just changed first. Be unemotional and unshaken around her even if you feel that way.

Be emotional and hurt when you're alone. Never let her see you emotional and breaking down because of her. You give her the feeling of having too much power over your life when she sees how her leaving affected you. Let her see you as a strong man who can't be played with emotionally.

Some women will break up with you just to see how you react. Just to test how far she has imprinted herself on your heart and emotions. To see if her leaving hurts you or not. Just move on to the next woman. No honorable man wants to look weak, especially because he's put all of his faith in a woman who makes decisions based upon her temporary emotions.

If you have real value then you'll have other options even if not immediately. Just get back to working on yourself. Use the fuel of her leaving for your good by becoming an even greater man that she'll be jealous of. Then get a better woman than her. Women date and marry to find the best option she has at that time.

If a man she thinks is a better option comes then she'll leave. This is the nature of a woman's biology to find the best mate for her. It's called hypergamy. This is why statistically women leave their marriages and relationships a majority of the time. And it's why she usually has a new man already when she leaves you.

Women build bridges to new men when she's unhappy in her present relationship. That's why women are quicker than most men to leave the relationship, so expect her to leave first. Be prepared for it financial and emotionally if she stays or goes. The best way to be prepared is to always be working hard to be a better version of yourself. In this way you will never lose.

Handling Conflicts

Her Domination Means Your Elimination

When you get comfortable in the relationship you let your guard down. This is when she'll test you into submission and go for the kill of your confidence and your masculine ego. If you pass her tests by standing up for yourself and speaking up strongly for how you want things to be done in the relationship, then you will gain her respect and her confidence in you.

But if you fail by being silent about your opinions, saying what you think she wants to hear so you'll avoid conflicts and getting along just to get along you'll lose her respect and her body over the length of the relationship. To prevent her relationship domination you have to always stay your solid masculine self from the beginning.

If you started the relationship being strong in your ways, stay strong even when she shows you her soft side. You can't give her 50% affection and 50% firmness, it must look more like 20-30% affection and 70-80% firmness. Each woman is different but 70% firmness and 30% affection is average.

Women have an instinct to strike when you're at your most vulnerable. This is why she can leave you and turn on you in a second because she wants to feel powerful over you. It's not because she's evil, it's that the yen which the woman represents is chaos. The yang is the male and represents order.

Any man who allows his order to descend into her chaos will experience misery and disorder in his life. One of the attributes of yen is darkness because there is a darkness that exists in all women. Just think about the women who've done you wrong in your past. Haven't they done things to you that you would've never done to them? Exactly!

You are the giving light, she is the dark accepting force. This is understanding the man and the woman at an energetic level. You are the sun and she is the moon. Why do you think that witches worship the moons energy? She can relate to the energy of the moon. That's because she's energetically built to absorb your light as the sun and moon work in mother nature.

The sun gives the moon light and the moon shines the reflection it has absorbed from the sun at night. So your job as a man is to never let a woman dim your light by taking more energy from you than you're willing to give. Because once she absorbs all of your light through her domination of you then she'll lose interest in you automatically.

There's nothing else she can gain from being with you anymore so she'll be gone with the wind. So before you even interact with a woman romantically you must have a line drawn in the sand about how far you'll give to her. Because she is the chaos element and she can bring you destruction if you give up all of your masculine energy to her.

For example, just look around you and count how many women are talking about their problems all the time. She revolves around chaos, she watches chaos on tv, on her phone, she worries about chaos happening to her and she'll bring a man chaos and disorder into his life by demanding every ounce of his attention if he gives it to her.

A woman will even create problems in the relationship if there aren't any problems due to her excessive thinking and chaotic mindset. She breaks a man down very methodically with control and by making small problems big problems. Every time you give in and give her, "her" way she loses a little respect for you and she gains a little more power in the process.

For example she doesn't always want the things that she's acting like she wants. She's just testing you to see if you'll give in and give it to her even though you don't want to. That's because it's just a woman's nature to test you to see how far you will go for her. Understand this will help you always keep a woman's respect.

Tell her "no" when you feel like telling her no. Don't just give in because you think it'll make her happy. She'll love you more if she can't get over on you. Because even if she moves on she'll still respect that you didn't fail her tests. If you stand on principles she will never forget you because most men will compromise their way into her dominance.

Simply because these men don't know what she's really doing she'll dominate them. She'll gain and keep her respect for you because of your strength to remain yourself. You never allowed her to dominate or steal your masculine light so she will see you as a strong and confident man over the men she easily dominated.

If a woman constantly tests you in areas of your life that she knows you won't compromise on, let her go. Let the relationship die because this type of woman wants to beat you into submission with her tests. She doesn't respect you because she's selfish and doesn't respect anybody especially men.

Some man in her past hurt her so much that she's developed severe trust issues and she's taking out her hurt on you. Her constant emotional tests are actually showing that she wants to defeat your masculinity and defeat your confidence so you can be weak mentally like she is. These women are a perfect example of toxic femininity.

Most women want to dominate strong men because she's obsessed with the desire to control a man. This makes her feel more powerful than a man in a culture where the man is looked at as the most powerful. She knows that she may not be able to defeat you physically but she has a great chance of defeating you emotionally and mentally.

When she does defeat a man mentally and emotionally she gets the feeling of strength and power from being able to beat him. Her best weapons against a man are her mind and her body. Because most men are weak to a woman sexually, she'll use her body and emotional manipulation to make a man weak.

This is why she withholds sex from a man. She wins mentally and sexually when she controls what a man desires the most. Most men elevate sex over everything so she easily defeats a man mentally by only giving him sex when "she" wants to.

A woman gets bored testing and dominating weak men, so she prefers strong men who she can break down because she feels more accomplished from it. She doesn't get any feeling of accomplishment from breaking weak men because they're already weak. It makes her feel empty after defeating a weak man because she doesn't get much energy from this man.

The more often she only defeats weak men the more she's burned out from dominating them. This is why there's so many unhappy and angry women. So to keep from being defeated by a woman don't waste time arguing and over explaining to a woman who doesn't listen. Because if she doesn't listen at any point of the relationship then she doesn't respect you.

If she doesn't listen to you then she's not the right woman to be in a relationship with anyway. Because if she can't break you down through arguing or withholding sex then she knows her manipulation won't work on you. Even when dealing with women you aren't in a relationship with, never let them dominate you.

If you're a disciplined man and none of the mental or sexual manipulation works on you, she'll be attracted to you out of curiosity. But always remember that her attraction to you is based upon her desire to change you, not her desire for you as you are. So once she gets you focused on her she will try her manipulation game.

Be smarter than her games and pick women who accept you as you are. A woman's need to control is deeply ingrained in her psyche and her energetic nature. Show her that the games won't work and you'll teach your woman to respect your manhood. You teach a woman how to treat you, but if you aren't careful she will use sexual and emotional manipulation to defeat you.

Don't Argue With Your Girl, Ever!

If you act like her by being overly emotional and argumentative then you're acting like a woman. Why does she want another woman when she picked you thinking that you were a man? Women want masculine energy because they don't have it themselves. Attraction is built off of energetic opposites.

You are masculine energy which is logical and not overly emotional. And she's feminine energy which is emotional but not overly logical. If you act like a woman's feminine energy by arguing and being over emotional, she will see you as another woman. This kills her attraction to you and destroys her respect for you as a man.

Emotional and feminine men attract masculine women. And masculine men attract feminine women. Mother nature built us to be attracted to our energetic opposite. So the energy that you are will attract the opposite energy of that which you are. For attraction to work then she has to see you as her energetic opposite.

So if you act feminine and submissive when dealing with her, then she'll naturally become dominant and masculine when dealing with you. All you have to do is look at a gay couple. They're under the same energetic principles of attraction. Is there not always a more masculine and feminine person in their relationship dynamics? Of course there is!

A masculine man can become a feminine man in the relationship by engaging in emotional arguments and by also becoming what "she" wants him to be in the relationship. Women are hardwired to treat you the way that you make her feel. So if you become feminine and submissive to her then she will automatically become masculine and dominant in the relationship.

This is why it's dangerous for any man in a romantic relationship to give a woman everything that she wants and put himself aside. By submitting to her demands, wants and needs you are letting her be the masculine energy in the relationship. And it's a very submissive and feminine act to let her dominate the demands and leadership in the relationship.

Because a woman will always relate energetically to you in the way you relate to her energetically by adapting to the relationships flow. For example, if you act like a woman around her she will see you and treat you as she would treat another woman. But if you act like a man she will see you and treat you like a man and take her place as a woman.

When you give her all of your obedience and attention by letting her run the flow of the relationship, then you're giving away for cheap your only value to her which is your masculine energetic attention. Your masculine energetic attention is what she craves or else she wouldn't need or desire a man in her life.

If you're fighting and arguing with her then you're giving her your masculine energetic attention. And in the process you become feminine energy. When you engage in arguments with your woman and you allow her to control your thoughts, steal your masculine energy and manipulate your emotional behaviors your attention becomes less valuable and less respected by her.

Anytime she wants to fight, you have 2 options:

<u>Option #1</u>: Tell her that you will NOT engage in petty arguments. When she can calm down and act like an adult then she can talk to you. Otherwise you have nothing to say to her.

<u>Option #2</u>: Hang up the phone or leave until she can talk to you with logic instead of emotions. You will NOT engage with any woman who is yelling, being rude or not behaving as if she wants to find a solution to the issue.

Regardless of how mad she gets, do not allow yourself to act upset, yell or say rude things back. This behavior will only feed her emotions at the time so she can make you the bad guy. Stay in your masculine energy. Using these options show her that you will not act feminine, also that she can't manipulate you through arguing to give her your masculine energy.

If she refuses to act like a feminine adult woman then you take away your attention until she does. This means that you have to be willing to lose her if she doesn't act right. The beautiful thing about staying in your masculine energy is that most of the time she won't leave. She'll submit to her feminine energy and come back to you using her logic and reasoning.

Arguing with a woman will never work out in your favor because she's fighting with emotions and you're fighting with logic. If you even start winning by using your emotions she'll just use more effective emotions like crying to get you to submit. She's used to manipulating a man with emotions so don't even fight in her arena of expertise.

Women have learned since young girls how to turn their emotions on and off to get their way. It started with her parents and then her boyfriends and friends, so she's a master at emotional manipulation. Even if she doesn't use the crying technique she'll dig and dig until she finds your soft spot with insults, guilt, blame or shame.

So the best technique for a man is to not even play the emotional game with her. Leave her to her own emotions until she gets tired of carrying them because she has nowhere to put them. Now she has to look herself in the mirror and face her emotions by herself because you're not going to accept them.

Once she sees that you can't be emotionally manipulated, then she'll be forced to use her logic. That's your natural area of expertise. Forcing her to get out of her emotions and deal with the issue using her logic puts her in a space where she has to deal with the reality of solid facts and ideas, not emotions. Emotion is based on nothing but feelings which are always changing.

The Formula:

A. If she tries to lure you into an emotional argument then use options #1 or #2 to take away your attention and her power

B. If she does good by stopping herself and tapping into her logic by calming down and being respectful then reward her with a lot of your attention. Listen to her and then do something nice for her.

C. If she doesn't become logical, respectful and she still tries to bait you into emotional agreements then leave or stay silent until she can be respectful. If she can't leave her, it's that simple.

It is your job as a man to be consistent and show her that you will not ever engage in a relationship with a woman who cannot or will not be respectful, logical or reasonable. Be consistent in your actions and if she learns to disagree respectfully, you've trained her how to disagree.

This is how a man keeps his masculine energy and keeps a woman around who has to be feminine to respect his masculinity. Some toxic feminine women love to see you angry, upset and feminine because it gives her the feelings of power over you. The more toxic she is the more she will try to poke and prod you into feminine disagreements.

Does she not gossip, fight with her friends, and watch fighting reality tv and gossip on tv? Of course she does because it fuels her feminine energy. Don't participate and you will find that she will either submit or quit. Either way you win!

Stay Ready & Willing To Walk Away

This applies to everything in life:

-Your job

-Friendships

-Relationships

-Family

Always be ready to walk away when your manhood is being disrespected or compromised. As a man anytime your self respect is being compromised to meet someone else's demands, you have to choose your dignity, your masculinity and walk away.

Relationships are the most common place that a man compromises his manhood and his self respect for his woman's wants, needs and desires. But this is extremely dangerous to a man's self esteem. For example, your woman gives you an ultimatum or says, "If you don't do this" then she'll leave you.

Or she's choosing between you and another man while you stick around wait for her to pick you hopefully. Most men submit to her demands and don't walk away with their power and manhood still intact when they should. You will always thank yourself later that you walked away with your power and self respect in the long run over anything.

If anyone is trying to push you to compromise your wants, needs and desires for theirs, then they already have a low level of respect for you. Since they already have a low level of respect for you, the only way to get it back is take your power and leave. When it comes to a woman she's not yours mentally or physically anymore when she starts giving you ultimatums.

When she starts trying to force you to do things you don't want to do just so she'll choose you then she's already halfway out the door. If you compromise your needs for her wants she'll lose all respect for you anyway. So you're better off taking your self respect and leaving her behind.

This is the only way to earn back her respect and keep your self respect at the same time. Once she sees that you'll compromise yourself because you're afraid that she'll leave you she'll see weakness. Once she sees that you're weak for her then the manipulation will get worse and more frequent over time.

Now she'll rely on this form of manipulation to get whatever she wants as leverage over you whenever you don't do what she wants you to do. The second you compromise yourself for her, that's the moment when you have now become her slave.

If you let her manipulate you into compromising yourself for her happiness, wants or her needs once, she'll try to get you to compromise again. Once you've compromised yourself once, she won't be happy until you compromise yourself again. Now she won't be happy until you compromise again because it got her what she wanted.

Understand that the second a woman tries to make you compromise your self respect and you do it, you lose her respect for your boundaries. So when you walk away from her and the relationship then you take your power back and show her that she can't control you with her one sided demands.

The compromise of your desires, opinions, thoughts, actions and beliefs will always equal her losing respect for you, and you losing respect for yourself. Now she sees that she can get you to do things that you don't want to do, so it's "Game Over" and you're the one who lost! You lost her attraction and her attention.

Rather you die like a man than live like a coward. Because when you bend over backwards for anyone out of compromise and you let them manipulate you, you'll lose more and more of their respect and your self respect every time.

This is the real meaning of selling your soul for something or someone. Always be willing to walk away quickly from whatever is trying to steal your self worth. The price you pay for giving in and compromising your manhood for anyone is 1000x worse than the pain of walking away and keeping your pride, dignity and manhood intact.

You'll always be proud of yourself that you walked away in the long run, versus how you would feel if you kept compromising. Be willing to walk away from even your dream girl if she gets manipulative and starts trying to get you to compromise for her.

Understand that any woman that tries to push you into compromising yourself to do things that they know you don't want to do, is only asking you because she doesn't want to compromise herself for you. In most cases the people asking you to compromise won't do the same for you. They'll never make themselves uncomfortable for your comfort, that's why they'll ask you to do it.

Your woman will never submit or compromise to an unfair expectation like she's asking you to. So why are you expected to compromise on things that she won't? Because she doesn't want to compromise herself and her self esteem for you.

She wants to see if she has the power in the relationship to make you submit and do the compromising. This is why as soon as she starts asking for you to compromise yourself for her and do things that you know she wouldn't do for you, you head straight out the door ready to leave for good if she doesn't apologize.

Why? Relationships are all about power and control. And women are great at using emotional and sexual manipulation to gain the control from men in relationships. Relationships are not some fairy tale idea of "love" built by cartoons and the media.

Relationships are built upon one person being more dominant and one person being more submissive. And women are great at gaining the dominant position over men in relationships because they feel like the prize in the relationship. This is due to society and due to men compromising themselves because they don't want her to leave.

Walking away from manipulative women and situations will always be more rewarding in the long term even if it hurts in the short term. Why? because you not only show her that you won't be sexually or emotionally manipulated, you'll keep her respect.

You will always gain a high level of respect for yourself by putting your happiness and your peace of mind first. Sacrificing your self respect to make anyone else happy will always leave you empty and broken. There's nothing or nobody that you can't live without. You are the only one that you can't live without.

Because when you compromise you for anyone or anything else, you kill your self esteem, your self worth and your self respect. If you compromise yourself for other people eventually you won't recognize yourself anymore. You'll leave wondering who am I? Because you compromised your needs, your wants, your desires and your manhood to make someone else happy.

Too many men stay and compromise their value and their self esteem for a woman hoping to keep the family together. This is because they believed the fairytale sold to men and women of soul mates and of a prince charming coming to rescue his princess.

The idea of finding the "one" pushes men to put these labels on unworthy women who are not the "one". The "one" doesn't exist in real life, only in his mind. But because he didn't want to let go of a fairy tale fantasy, he compromises himself more than he can afford to. This is why so many men are unhappy in relationships today!

Understanding Emotional Manipulation

Emotional manipulation comes in two forms:

#1. Trying to get you upset because she's upset from a bad day, inner turmoil or a bad mood

#2. Withholding sex and sexual pleasure because she wants you to behave as she wants you to behave to earn sex or sexual favors from her

Misery loves company and because she's in a bad mood because of something, she'll take it out on you to ruin your happiness so you're both unhappy together so she feels better. An angry person cannot be comfortable around a happy and cheerful person. The angry person will try to pull you down into the angry level so that they can feel better about being angry.

So it is key that you remain detached and objective from her emotional game. When you're objective and not tied into her emotional state by thinking it's your job to make her happy, you'll easily be able see what game she's trying to pull you into. This is the time to give her comfort and allow her to express her emotions and talk about what's really the root of these emotions.

You can't make her happy because it's not your job. But you can be her emotional stability if she accepts it, if not leave. It's very important that you don't allow yourself to be caught up and "hooked" into her negative energy simply because her words or actions pushes the angry button in you.

Recognize the emotional manipulation game she's trying to play and refuse to play along by getting angry, upset of frustrated that she's in a negative mood. She's in control of her emotions, not you! The fix to the problem is not to try and fix it at all. She has to fix her own emotions.

If she tells you what's her issue don't get mad at who she's mad at or accept her negative emotions, stay calm and objective. You're not here to fix her problems and this thinking helps you stay objective and non over emotional. You can support her but you cannot fix or change any of her emotions that have nothing to do with you.

By consistently being objective you'll show her that you will not play emotional manipulation games. You won't get mad just because she's mad. And she will eventually learn that you won't be easily pulled into fights or drama. Sexual manipulation is also a form of emotional manipulation.

Why? because she's using something that you enjoy and weaponizing it against you to get an emotional reaction out of you. She knows that you'll respond negatively to her not giving you sex because men enjoy the pleasure of sex. Once she sees how you react she'll either keep using your desire for sex to make you do what she wants or she'll withhold sex just to make you upset.

This is very common in longer term relationships because often a woman isn't sexually attracted to you like before, so she doesn't crave sexual contact from you anymore. So she uses your desire for sex to manipulate your behaviors. When she tries to weaponize sex with her as sexual manipulation never beg or act like her sex is more valuable than your sex.

If she tries to manipulate you emotionally through sex then you only have 2 solutions:

#1. Tell her that you will not be manipulated sexually, and if she wants to play these kinds of immature games, you will NOT stay in the relationship!

#2. Leave the relationship because sex should never be weaponized if she enjoys it too! Leave because she's either not sexually attracted to you anymore or having sex with someone else.

How To Manipulate A Combative Woman

The "Stroke Her Ego" Strategy

All that runs the mind of a combative woman is her ego. She wants her ego to be validated at all times for her to feel secure in herself. That's why if you don't agree with her every time, she feels like she has to fight to be right for her own validation.

The Technique:

To deal with a combative woman all you have to do is agree with whatever she's saying as a form of passive aggressive manipulation. It's that simple! Don't get angry, agree with her more. It'll make her upset but keep it up. When she says something negative towards you, just agree more without attaching yourself to her angry emotions.

When you agree with her regardless of how insulting she tries to get, it only hurts her and makes her more angry. What this does scientifically is it diffuses the negative energetic attack that she's trying to hit you with. You're deflecting her anger and negativity with your armor of passiveness.

So she'll try to make you even more mad by being more insulting and vicious. This is the time to be listening very closely to what she's saying in anger, because this is what she really feels inside. Anger opens the doorway to hateful words but also the inner truth someone holds. You get to hear her honest emotions because she's saying how she's feeling to hurt you.

But she's speaking "her mind" to you. So listen closely! When most people get angry they will immediately start throwing darts meant to stir up anger and dissension in you. This works in your favor because you get to hear how people really feel about you deep inside. This is how you get to see their full and uncensored self on display.

Now you can evaluate if this person is who you really want to be with or not. This is why you listen closely to what they have to say. They've shown their cards to you while you get to keep yours. This will always work in your benefit. If you're not with them you get to see how quality of a person they are because they're out of their own emotional control. Now act upon what you know!

Handling Conflict With Baby Mothers

Her actions and reactions will always change once you break up so expect it! Because when a woman is hurt, especially if you hurt her she'll show you a different degree of feelings that weren't present when you were with her. You can't be mad at her, especially if you hurt her first, forgive her for being angry at you.

And then understand that she's going to be determined to make you feel hurt like she is. Even if you aren't remorseful act like you are. Because the more you act like you don't care that she's hurt, the more she's going to want to hurt you. This is human psychology. Hurt people, hurt people.

If you validate the energy of her feelings she can't stay hurt. But if you don't validate her feelings she will keep trying to get you to. That's because there's nothing more vengeful than a woman scorned. So the more that you act like she's done something to you, or act jealous of her new relationship the worse it will get for you.

You have to take a way her power to hurt you by disempowering the energy of her anger. You disempower negative energy by doing things that diffuse that energy out of a person. And you'll defuse her negative energy by not giving her a place to put her anger anymore. Now so she has to deal with it herself.

All she's going to do is let it go over time because it's uncomfortable for her to hold that negative energy without a person to give it to. If you refuse to accept it by diffusing and deflecting it then you will over time get your way with her. Don't stay the outlet of her negative energy by making it worse and denying your part in the breakup.

Just accept it so you don't have to keep playing her blame game. Your main goal is to keep contact with your child, remember that! You give a woman too much power over you when she sees that she can say things to make you angry because she's hurt. Even if you weren't the reason for the breakup, by giving her the power to hurt you it makes her feel more powerful than you.

And if she sees that she can hurt you easily, then she will always attempt to get you to act out of character. Women run off of emotions. The more negative emotions you give her, the more she'll use them as the fuel to blame you for her own emotional issues. Most women don't have the power to control their emotions.

So whenever you let her get you emotional and in your feelings, she has manipulated you to get on her emotional level, instead of you manipulating her to get on your higher logic level. So whenever you see her in her negative emotions don't overreact and fuel her feelings by giving her back negative emotions.

Your job is to keep her respect so you can have access to your child or children. So to keep her respect you have to always stay out of your emotions. Because what she'll do is tell your children that you're the problem. Then she'll tempt you into getting emotional in front of the children and you'll look like the bad guy.

Children will see the viewpoint of whoever has the most access to their minds. So if the children are with her then she'll tell them all of the bad things you've done while never mentioning how she participated or tempted you purposely to be angry. So stop reacting to her emotional assaults even if you know she's wrong.

There's no convincing her of her ways, ever. This is where most men fail when dealing with the mother of their child. They try to fight her emotions with emotions. It never works! You have to stay in your logic because that's where she has a hard time keeping up with you mentally.

Stay focused on your position as a father and remind her when she tries to tempt you int an argument that you're only focused on being there for your child. She'll try over and over to make you angry until she sees that it doesn't work anymore. This is how a man handles a woman in all situations.

Eventually she will see that no matter what game she plays, your focus is on being a father to your child. Always maintain a calm, cool and non emotional demeanor. Always be a man who is unshakeable and cannot be persuaded into petty fights and arguments just because she's angry at you for the relationship not working anymore.

No woman has to be a certain type of woman in order for you to be a certain type of man. You must always remain a man regardless of ANY woman's actions. If she sees you acting emotional like her she will never respect you because you're acting 100% just like she is by nature, like a woman. If you can't get access to your children take her to court!

Child support is better than losing your mental, physical and emotional peace in any way. Being able to focus on a new woman, your goals and your next moves is better than dealing with stress and turmoil from anyone. Be a man and go get more money! Use her anger against her and transform her negative energy into you going out and becoming more successful than she dreamed of.

This is energy manipulation. Success is always the greatest revenge! Stay two steps ahead of her and don't tell her what you're doing to gather evidence about her keeping the kids away from you if she is. Document and record any negative calls she makes and be cool while she makes a fool of herself.

Stay logical and strategic when dealing with a woman, especially an angry woman who wants to hurt you. You will always win if you stay logical while she is emotional. Emotional people don't think their actions through fully, so they make big mistakes.

Your goal has to stay and always be focused on being the best father you can to your children. When she sees that you're progressing in your life past her and growing in your maturity, she will have to level up or stay in her feelings. Either way you win!

Understanding Female Mind Manipulation

Female Sexual Mind Manipulation

Women learn and understand since young girls how to mentally and emotionally manipulate men. And they learn that a man's #1 weakness is his desire for sex. Because a man's desire for sex is so strong and hard for him to control he becomes easy prey to her curves and smooth words.

A man is so easily manipulated by his sexual desires that the media, women and marketing convert it into money. For examples, Only fans, porn, strip clubs, hooters restaurants, beer companies, music and entertainment, sports, etc. The porn industry alone is a billion dollar business built off of a mans desire for sex.

Millions of men exchange their hard earned money to women in the sex industry just because the spirit of a mans desire for sex is so strong. So in a man's life it becomes incredibly important that he realizes how his sexual nature is being manipulated by women and the media to control, direct and stimulate his primal urges and impulses for their gain instead of his.

Once a man recognizes that his sexual desires are being manipulated by women and everyone else looking to make money off of him, he can place sexual discipline upon himself. He has to learn to stop thinking with his dick and think with his brain. It's a mans desire that leads his life.

Desires are at the root of a man's existence, because they pull him, they push him and they motivate him to gain whatever he wants in life. The desires a man pursues will either be beneficial to his life once they are fulfilled or those desires will end up detrimental to the quality of his life, his mind and his body once fulfilled.

But in terms of a man's desire for sex when it comes to women, you must become very careful to not get manipulated by her ability to turn on your desires for sex to get her way with you. A woman's game is very simple because they're built to attract men. That's why they have curves, soft voices and feminine energy.

Without her ability to attract you by looking pretty or having a sexy shape she wouldn't have so much power over a mans mind. So this is the only strategy a woman has to get a man. This is the key for a man to understand so he has the right mindset to beat a woman at her own game. Understand emotional manipulation is her only move on the chess board.

But it's a very powerful move because it gets you distracted by using your desires against you. You get distracted by her body, her makeup, her feminine voice, the thought of sex and the thought of even making her your wife. But the whole time she used all of these tools against you. This is the art of female manipulation.

For example, you'll see a pretty woman who's incredibly attractive to you and automatically you'll think that she's so awesome inside which happens for many men.

This is referred to as the "Halo Effect". Men think that they're so amazing inside and out because they're beautiful, cute or pretty.

But in reality she might be emotionally immature, needy, angry and sometimes even physically abusive. This is why as a man you have to start looking past your desire to sleep with her and start paying closer attention to how her mind works. This is the only way you can beat her very powerful game of emotional manipulation.

Because when you gain a woman in your life, you don't just get a woman's body, you get her mind. Beauty without character has to means nothing to you in this game of dating, women and sex. If you're the easily manipulated man that sex is all you're after, just like the female black widow spider first attracts her prey and then catches her prey, then kills him after, you're dead.

Dead end relationships, dead sexual attraction and sometimes even physical death is all you can get out of a woman who has learned how to take her male manipulation techniques to the levels of mastery. The issue is the most cunning, strategic, cold hearted and manipulative women are often the most beautiful and the most attractive.

This is because they've had so much practice with different types of men to perfect her strategies. This is why it's do important to play the game differently than most of the men she'll meet. Take the time to learn her character. And don't be so quick to have sex with a woman just because your dick wants to.

Play the game differently than 99% of men by being the one who controls the sexual interactions because sex plays right into her hands and right into her male manipulation. Your super power is in what she's trying to earn from you, which is a relationship. Women control access to sex and men control access to relationships.

This means that you as a man can't just grab any girl and have sex with her without you going to jail. You have to get her permission to access her body sexually. Her only super power is sex. So she tries to give you sex in exchange for a relationship with you. All you have to do is act like you don't want sex as bad as most men before you and you're now the manipulator, instead of her.

Make her work for your sex instead of you working for hers and you're now playing the game in a way that takes her power away. She now has to earn your commitment and the privilege of being in a relationship with you. She'll lose her mind because she actually has to do some work outside of sex to earn your attention.

It's been so easy with men before you because all she had to do was lay on her back and let them do all of the work, while she wins the game of manipulation to get each man hooked. He got easily manipulated by his own desire for sex and fell in love with her body instead of her mind, her body, and her attitude.

This is why later in the relationship when her sex got old he opened his eyes and finally sees who she really is. But it's too late because he's been manipulated into giving her the position of power. He married her, gave her his loyalty or fell in love with her and now she has access to his money, his resources and if not his things, his emotions.

This is why you have to first be aware of who she really is and how she really thinks besides her body. Regardless of how beautiful the outside parts of a woman may be, if her mind isn't right, open the door and let her return from where she came. This is why you can't ever try to fix traumatized, unhappy or emotionally broken women.

You'll always find yourself on the losing end in the process of trying to save her from herself and her chaotic mind. A woman's mind is the most precious resource that a man can have. But if her mind is negative, destructive and miserable, then she can only bring you nothing but pain and heartache.

The 4 Roles Women Use Men For

Women look for a man to fit her needs, there's nothing else to it. And unlike a man sees a woman, she doesn't need you for sex. She just uses a mans desire for sex to lure him into her life to fill the bigger overall lacking need she's looking to fill.

So before you get lured in by your own desire and lust for sex, stop and take a moment to look at her life and see what she's lacking at in her life at this time. What lack in her life is she trying to fill with your presence? There's always at least one area in her life that's lacking. There are only 4 areas that she's trying to fulfill with having a man in her life.

The fact that she's lacking in at least one of these areas is always why she's looking for a man in the first place. A woman lives her life led by her emotions. So each of these 4 areas she's seeking to fulfill are all emotionally based needs. These emotional needs that she wants you to fix in her life will always be temporary.

So understand that once you fill that emotional need in her life for the time being, filling another emotional need will become the priority in her life. And no one man can fill every emotional need in a woman's life at the same time. So that means that for her there will be no need to keep you in her life anymore.

It will be time for her to find another man to fill a different emotional need that she needs in her life. This is why she calls that new desire for a new emotional need to be met as her "happy." This just means that she is desiring a new emotional need to be met in her life.

For example, if you're there to fill her emotional need as a provider financially for her and her children, then you'll only be needed until the kids are 18 and on their own. Once it just becomes you and her in the house alone, her emotional need for you as a provider for the children is gone, so the relationship starts going downhill.

How many relationships have you heard of dismantle once the kids were grown and gone? Many right? Her emotional need for a provider gets replaced by her emotional need for excitement and freedom. This new emotional need will bring the desire for the "fun guy" to take your place because you're the responsible and loyal but boring dad type.

So understanding which emotional need a woman desires in her life for you to fill, will determine the length of time you'll be around. After that emotional need ends for her, she'll be gone to fill the next emotional need.

A Woman's 4 Emotional Needs:

Role #1: A Short Term Fix For A Painful Past

Your presence in her life serves as a distraction from her emotionally draining mind and life. Her mental and sometimes physical life is chaotic so she needs you to be a band aid in her life. You're the man she tells all of her problems to and cries about them with. She just broke up from a bad relationship or she's still in one and she needs someone to vent and dump her emotions on.

She lost someone special to death, was sexually molested early in her life, had a bad parenting experience, she was picked on, bullied, has a negative outlook on life in general or had abusive relationships because of picking "bad boys". You're in her life to tell her that everything will be okay.

And you serve as a safe and secure place in her life and as a distraction from herself until she feels better about herself or her past. These relationships last the shortest amount of time because once she dumps all of her emotional baggage on you she needs a new person to give her safe and secure validation.

Trying to fix a damaged and broken woman emotionally always backfires on a man because you will never be able to save a woman from herself and her own mind. All you'll find in the process is frustration, anger and disappointment. She is who she wants to be, remember that!

<u>Key Attributes</u>: Very needy emotionally and always talks about her pain or who hurt her. It's always them who hurt her, it's never her fault. This keeps her from taking responsibility and healing the pain she holds on to.

Role #2: As The Fun Guy

You serve as someone she can just let go of her emotions and have fun with. She calls on you for sex, she calls you to talk for hours and laugh, but she doesn't see you as marriage material because you're just the fun guy. She may have just left a serious and hard on her emotional relationship.

She could have just left a long term relationship, an abusive relationship or she's just a young woman looking to have fun until the guy she really wants comes around. These women don't take life seriously because she's young or just had to be serious and responsible in her life.

So she looks for a man who just wants to party, have irresponsible sex with and engage with her emotionally in a very fun and energetic way. The need to just have fun is a short phase in her life because women are usually more advanced than a man when it comes to responsibility.

She knows that you're not very responsible but she knows that you'll both have a lot of fun together. This is often why she picks the bad guys in this phase of her life. She doesn't take the bad guy serious enough for a relationship because he's not responsible, but his irresponsibility is exactly what makes him fun.

With young women, they usually make the mistake of having children with these men. While enjoying his irresponsible nature and her own irresponsible actions she gets pregnant. Now because he's the irresponsible fun guy, he's not a suitable father.

This is when her time with the fun guy starts to come to an end. Now she needs to have her emotional need for the next guy to be filled. She desires the emotional need for the provider man who will take care of the child and her financially.

<u>Key Attributes</u>: Party animal who always has a drink, drugs or both around because she doesn't want to think at all, she just wants to feel good. She wants to party or do anything to have fun. Sitting at home for her is boring and not interesting. She wants to move!

Role #3: As A Provider For Her And Her Kids

A man who can come in and be the "Man" example and provider for the family because she's overwhelmed without one. She's tired of leading, feeding and providing for the kids by herself, so she wants to have help with all of her responsibilities.

She likely had a child or children with extremely underdeveloped men like the "fun guy" who weren't responsible to be fathers for the children. Or she's emotionally broken and left the previous men due to her emotional immaturity. So now she's looking to have her emotional need filled of a protector and a provider for her and the children.

She's looking for a security guard and a financial provider, instead of providing her own financial and physical security. These are the baby mamas and the single mothers of the world who are always complaining about men, yet need a man in her life at the same time. That's because she's hurt by the men in her past, but she still wants a man for his benefits to make life easier.

These women can sometimes make great wives, until the kids grow. But once they grow the emotional needs she wants and desires from a man changes. Instead of a steady and responsible man, she'll want the fun guy again who is about fun and excitement. That's because she's had to be responsible for a length of time. She'll crave the freedom of emotional actions.

<u>Key Attributes</u>: Family women and single mothers who are looking for a male provider for her family. She may be independent minded herself but her goal is to make sure her kid has a man in their life. She wants to feel safe and secure so she picks a provider.

Role #4: As A Building Project

She sees you as a flawed and imperfect man who needs her fixing and changing. So she wants to mold you and fix you into who she sees your potential to be in her mind. Her female need for control and her ego wants to make you better than you are like she's raising a child.

She feels like if she can change you into a better man, she can make you the perfect man for her.

She looks for an insecure guy or a rough around the edges guy who can be changed into her "perfect guy". He needs to be changed because he's either a bad guy or he's a nerdy and low confidence level man who has the potential to look better and talk better. So she tries to improve his looks and improve his swagger like he's one of her barbie and ken dolls.

Once she feels like she's changed him into a better man or she can't change him because he's resistant to her changes, she gets bored with him because he's not a better man like she thought he would be. He is still who he was from the beginning of the relationship.

And it frustrates her that her nagging, manipulation and constant suggestions for him to change aren't working to make him into who she sees in her head for him to become. So instead of accepting that her ego and her emotional need was to change him, she blames him for not being "man enough" for her and she leaves the relationship.

The real issue was her emotional need to feel like she has the power to change a man into her perfect guy. She didn't accept him for who he was, but she blames him for not being strong enough to handle her constant manipulation of him to change himself for her.

<u>Key Attributes</u>: She's very confident in her ability to communicate, but she's emotionally immature and overly opinionated. She doesn't listen well, but she talks a lot. She's always criticizing, gossiping about and judging everyones flaws but her own. She picks men who have less than her financially so she can be the one in charge.

A Woman's "All In, All Out" Strategy

This is where a woman uses her sex, her actions, and her attitude to make you think that she's a perfect woman who's wife material. She does this by putting her best foot forward and does the things that she knows you want but isn't really her actual self. So she puts in a lot of effort to get your attention at first and then it fades over time.

She shows her true self as she gets more comfortable doing what she wants, regardless if it's consistent with what she did before or not. So she doesn't show her true attitude when she's upset, she has sex with you a lot and often, caters to your wants, your needs and your desires, acts patient and understanding, listens and displays her best self at all times. Until she gets you!

The reality is that she did all of this to get your full attention, while never intending on keeping up these behaviors after she gets your full relationship attention.

It was all an act just to get you into a relationship with her. This all in, all out strategy a woman uses is why most marriages end with the woman.

In the beginning of the relationship, she put a tremendous amount of energy in and then stopped once she had her man. This is a similar strategy to the bait and switch. Once the man sees and notices that she's not acting the same as the beginning of the relationship, or doing the same things that she did in the beginning he feels deceived and played.

This plays into the fears of most men when it comes to women. A man's biggest fear in a relationship is that the woman he committed to will change on him because it happens so often, especially after a marriage. This is because once they're married, she's now feeling like she doesn't have to compete anymore for his commitment, so comfort and familiarity sets into the relationship.

She won the ultimate goal of his long term commitment, so there's nothing to work for anymore. This is when things start to go downhill for the relationship. Men think she's the "one" in the beginning because of the "all in" part of her strategy. Her initial high amount of effort in the beginning convinces him that he's found the "one" because she acts so perfect for him.

Because she was so "all in" in the beginning of them meeting each other and in the start of their romantic relationship, he believed that she's going to keep up this high amount of work, throughout the lifetime of the relationship. But he's been manipulated and tricked into believing in the fantasy that she sold to him.

All of her initial work was just meant to get him committed, so she can get comfortable that he won't leave her quickly. She simply set the bait out until she got you hooked on her line. Then once she was sure that you were hooked other line she reeled you in and threw you on the boat. Now that she has you hooked, she can become her true self.

Because her amount of work fades over time and she starts to act like the real her, men feel like they've been tricked and become dissatisfied with the relationship. This is why so many men cheat because they feel trapped until they cheat and release the pressure. A man wants a woman to be herself so he knows what he's getting when he gets her, just like she does.

So always take your time with a woman. And don't give her the privilege of a relationship until she has shown you who she really is. Pay attention to how she reacts when she's mad, when she's sad, when she's angry with you and when she has difficult life situations or relationship issues to deal with.

Tell her to do now, in the beginning of you being together, the things that she's going to keep up with in the relationship. And if she's doing something that she doesn't intend on keeping up in the relationship to stop. If you set this standard and have this conversation in the beginning you have built a foundation of expectations with her.

Then if she stops doing something "she" said she would keep up, then it's on her because it just exposes her laziness. Marriage to you has to be earned after she shows consistency in her attitude, her behaviors and in her habits, especially sexually. Any changing up will immediately warn you that she's using the "all in, all out" strategy just to get you hooked.

Women Use Seduction To Weaken You

Seduction Tools:

-The walk

-The tone of her voice

-The look up and down

-The hair toss

-The deep stare

-The question with the stare

These are tools she uses to manipulate you and defeat your logic so she can move you in the direction she chooses. A woman has no other way to get you hooked than seduction. Seduction is her only weapon. And women have learned how to easily seduce a man by using his ego against him.

So she uses her eyes, her body language and her sexy outfits to draw in your attention to her hypnotizing allure just to appeal a man's desire to be liked, admired and loved. So she uses compliments, physical touch and controlled but manipulative fake submission to disarm your mind into believing the illusion that she's selling you.

So like a trick falls for the dream a ho is selling him, you fall in love with a fantasy. You fall in love with the fantasy that she's yours and that she's into you much more than she really is. She only does this to disarm your barriers of mistrust because her game is to get behind your mental defense system.

She knows that if she can get past your mental defense system, she can start manipulating your mind to gain power over you. Once she gets past your mental defense system and convinces you of her worth through seduction, she gets your mind and imagination working. Now you start thinking about her when she's away, and you start thinking about how sex would feel with her.

You start feeling like you're privileged to have her in your life and that she's so amazing. But in reality, it's simply just a trick to get you hooked by using your lust against you to gain mental leverage in her favor. Once she gets you open through her seduction strategy, you'll strive to satisfy your desire for sex with her and you'll lose your logic. But this plays perfectly into her hands.

Now your mind is open and you're emotionally vulnerable to her body and her commands. Now you'll compromise yourself just to satisfy your desire to have sex with her. You'll start to monitor your words to stay on her good side just to make sure sex is still on the table.

What you've now done is pedestalized your idea of having sex with her, which is temporary, over truly getting to know who she really is. Have you ever been in a relationship with a woman and later wondered how you got in this situation with a girl who has completely switched on you with how she acts? This is why.

She used her female powers of seduction to get your imagination going, and she sold you a dream of who she seduced you into thinking she was, instead of who she really is in reality. Now you're more in love with your imaginative idea of who she could be than who she really is.

After you've had sex with her enough you snap back into reality, but its to late, she's tricked you into committing to her. She's gotten what she wanted from you and that's your commitment. Women control the access to sex and men control access to relationships in most cases.

The only time a woman controls both is when she's dealing with a weak and submissive man. This is why she uses her seduction to weaken you into giving her access into your mind to control both. Your temporary desire to have sex with her lets her trick you into trading something that's not as valuable to her, which is sex, for something that she truly values, which is a man's commitment.

Once she has you "by the balls" she takes the power position in the relationship. Because you submitted your value which is her access to your commitment, for the idea of your access to her sex. But you forget that she will always control your access to her sex until she decides that she doesn't want to give it to you anymore.

As soon as she decides that you don't deserve her sex anymore, now you realize that you made a big mistake. But by that time she's already taken advantage of your weaknesses and drained you of your emotional energy and also gotten access to your financial resources at that point.

She also completely drained your self esteem, your masculinity and your confidence, and now there's nothing for her to gain anymore. And when there's nothing to gain from you anymore, her attraction to you also dies in the process. She has slowly sucked the life out of you through her seductive manipulation technique.

This is why a woman ends the relationship and now you feel like you've lost yourself. You have, you've completely given in to her and traded your self worth for sex. Women all over the world use this same seduction until reduction strategy to gain access to not only a man's relationship, but also access to a mans resources quickly, especially financially.

Strip clubs, only fans, prostitutes and porn websites are the perfect examples of the seductive woman using seduction until reduction to gain access to a man's most valuable resources. Most women just use a "web"site and wait to catch men who are looking to trade for her sexual energy in exchange for his financial energy.

She doesn't even have to step outside to benefit from a man in her life, now she can benefit from many men at once. This is why it's important for a man to stop looking at dating apps, porn sites, social media babes, etc. because he's priming his mind to be manipulated by the next attractive woman that crosses his path.

He's priming his desire and lust for sex because he's already giving it to women online for free. So the next attractive woman that wants his resources and access to a relationship will already be in the perfect position to take advantage of him sexually. So whenever you deal with a woman you like, put your desire for sex with her after getting to know her mind.

This is how you can avoid getting played by her seductive ways. When a woman enters into your life, you don't just get her body you get her mind. Her body will only give you pleasure for a moment, but her mind can give you pain for a lifetime.

The 3 Stages Of Nagging You Into Submission

<u>Stage #1</u>: She'll pressure you through nagging into being perfect for her so that you can cater to her needs, her desires and her wants until you do exactly what she wants, how she wants it.

She'll also use passive aggressive, rude and condescending comments in the same way. They are all used for the same purpose of weakening your confidence and your self esteem enough so you'll stop fighting back her demands and just give in.

<u>Stage #2</u>: Once you submit to her authority and her ways of doing things because you want to keep her pussy available to you, she'll give you less of it as another form of control. Now you have to earn her sex unlike before.

If you don't do what she likes, when she likes it and how she likes it you to do things she'll create a fight out of it by making it a bigger issue than it is. This is all just a simple form of control to get you to stop

Stage #3: Then, after she gets you to submit to her demands full through sexual and emotional control, she'll leave you because you've become too boring and predictable to be fun anymore.

You've become controlled and easily manipulated so you now pose no challenge to her. This is why she loses her sexual attraction to you because it's your masculinity you had in the beginning that she was attracted to. But now it's gone! So is her interest!

Most women choose a man with the desire in mind to change him into who he can be instead of accepting who he is today. That's because most women pick men for their potential and not the actual reality of who they are.

Bad guys or alpha men in concept are just men who stay resistant to her nagging and urgings to change. They pose as a challenge to her because they don't give up who they are just because a woman wants them to change.

This is why she stays interested in these types of men because they aren't easily conquered and dominated without fighting back. They stand up for themselves and therefore demand respect because they won't allow her to conquer their masculinity.

This means that you can never give in to her nagging, passive aggressiveness, rude comments or any of her repetitive suggestions to change yourself for her if you want a woman to stay interested in you.

This doesn't mean be rude and rebellious, but it does mean always stand up for yourself and your beliefs without compromise. And if she can't give you the respect of speaking to you kindly and respecting you for who you want to be in life, then leave her behind.

You can never win by submitting who you want to be, in exchange for who she wants you to be. Because not only will you lose yourself in the process, you'll lose your self respect, your individuality, your masculinity and eventually her desire for you in the process.

2 Strategies Women Use To Control You

Strategy #1: With "Her" Attractiveness

She uses her feminine allure to work men into submission through sexual seductive body language, ego soothing words and physical touch. The more unattractive he is, the more likely he'll fall for just any woman's attractiveness. Ugly, low self confident and unattractive men are easier to control in most cases because they have less options.

This is why so many attractive women pick less attractive men to be with because he is easily controlled to do what she wants him to. He's easily manipulated and controlled because of his fear of losing her beauty and access to her pussy. An attractive woman is like having a trophy to a man, especially an unattractive or unconfident man.

He loves the feeling of being able to flaunt her beauty and attractiveness around for others to see and be jealous of his prize. This is just like an unconfident man with a lot of money or a beautiful car. These things help boost his low self esteem.

Just to be with her, he puts up with all of her mind games and manipulation because he's so scared of losing her and the social status and approval he gets from having an attractive woman around his arm. She knows he's wrapped around her finger and that he won't leave easily because he'll probably never get a more attractive woman than her.

This leads to her feeling a sense of power in the relationship. So she knows she can get away with a lot of very manipulative games to gain control of him, his actions, his beliefs and the relationship as a whole. She easily knows that she's in control.

Next time you see a very attractive woman and an unattractive man together in a relationship, pay very close attention to her choice of words and the body language she uses when you see them interacting together. Ask yourself who's in control? Who's leading the energy of the relationship? And who's the most valuable one in the relationship?

Men want the most attractive woman that they can get. So it's easy for an attractive woman to have all of the power in the relationship. A woman that is extremely attractive brings out the simp in even the best men because of their fear of losing her attractiveness and beauty.

A woman who knows how to manipulate a man's desire for sex because of her attractiveness, and understands the power of her beauty can defeat even the most masculine of men. So an unattractive man is much easier for her to control and manipulate. Even when a gold digger uses her power of beauty correctly, she doesn't even have to give him sex.

She can just lead a man on by selling him the fantasy of "maybe" having sex "later" after he gives her access to his money, his time, and his material possessions. Just the thought of maybe getting sex from her "later" is enough to get what she wants from him, because most men don't have dick control. Most men value pussy over their hard earned money and material possessions.

Strategy #2: With "Her" Money

Many modern day women make more money than their man or control the finances and the bills, so she has the financial power and the power of access to pussy over her man. Money is the easiest way to exert her power especially if she's not attractive. Many women purposely pick men with lower incomes because she knows that she can control him with her money.

This is also why so many women especially unattractive women who make a lot of money often avoid men with higher incomes than her. Because there's no way to control a man who doesn't need anything from her. If he's more attractive than her and has more money than her, she's less likely to get with him.

That's because now she can't control these types of men with money and sex. He already has money and he can get women because he's attractive, so now she has no leverage over him to use for control. A rich man has a lot to offer other women. So he won't deal with her controlling behaviors in any way.

Because she can control a man who makes less money than her so easily she'll move a guy with nothing into her home, just so she can control him with her money. This is why so many high earning women pick poor or underdeveloped men. She takes care of these men just to feel powerful.

But she won't stay attracted sexually to these men because she's only in the relationship for the power and to feel secure. So a man has to be totally independent of a woman to stay in control. If he lets her attractiveness push him to say and do things that give her the power in the relationship, he will always lose control of the relationship to her.

Never be focused at all on a woman's money or what she has to offer sexually or financially. Always have the attitude that her money or her attractiveness means nothing to you, regardless of how attractive she is or how much money she has.

To do this you must:

#1: Have dick control

#2: Have your own money

Women Prey On Your Weaknesses

From the beginning of the relationship she's trying to find your weaknesses and your vulnerabilities. That's because this is how women work. Women want to see what weaknesses they can use in a man to gain the balance of power in the relationship.

It's not because she's evil or some sort of bad person trying to take you down, she's just trying to find her edge in the relationship to feel powerful. A woman understands that she can't beat a man physically, so her battle ground is mental.

So she'll test you to see how you react to the things she throws at you that she can use to her advantage to get you off balance emotionally and mentally. She watches closely to how you react to her seduction, the boundaries she breaks and the words she says.

Some relationship experts and dating coaches often refer to the tests she throws your way as "shit testing". She'll take shots at your ego, your self esteem and do certain things that she knows will get different reactions out of you. While she's doing this testing she's taking note of which words make you sad, angry or happy and which words help her to get her way.

The whole time she's looking for what words and actions build you up and what words and actions tear you down. The way that you respond to her during these tests will reveal to her your strengths and your weaknesses. She wants to know if she can open you up through your ego and if can she open you up through your body?

Once she figures out which weaknesses you have she now knows the easiest way to get her way out of you. That's because women have extremely fragile ego's and can't handle the rejection of being told "no" like a man does. Men get told no all of the time and have to deal with rejection since young boys.

Women are rarely told no because people don't want to hurt their feelings. So in a woman's brain, the word "no" brings more pain to a woman's ego than it does a man's ego. So instead of risking being told "no" she will use these weaknesses she finds in you to get what she wants out of you.

This is simply a form of mental and physical manipulation used by most women, especially when it comes to men. For example, a woman can be in a relationship with you and tell you "no, not tonight" in your sexual advances, but if you tell her "no, not tonight", she'll become extremely aggravated, angry or passive aggressive towards you.

You're expected to take that rejection like a man, but she won't be able to accept that same rejection, from you without making sure that you feel some type of pain in return. Due to a woman's internal fear of rejection most women will manipulate their man for what they want before just asking a man straight forward for what she wants.

That's because manipulating you out of what she wants using your weaknesses gives her better odds of getting what she wants. There's also much more of a benefit for her ego when she can manipulate your weaknesses because it makes her feel powerful. For a woman, the less she gives and the more she gets, the more powerful in the relationship she feels.

She wants to feel like she has an advantage over you in the relationship at least emotionally or mentally to feel like she's at least your equal or above you. Feeling below you is hard for her ego to take because it frustrates her when a man dominates the power mentally and physically in the relationship. That's because she can't get her way from that type of man easily.

Why do you think that most women avoid extremely smart and educated men? It's because an extremely educated man in terms of mental, emotional and physical strength doesn't let her dominate and control the relationship like she wants to. Just watch a group of boy and girl kids playing together.

Who is the one giving the instructions and determining the activities they're going to play? The girls of course, especially if there's more than one. I use this example because children are the most pure in their mental and emotional nature.

And children don't have the developed manipulation techniques adults have, so they run off of the basic urgings that adults have learned to disguise. But in reality it is all the same. She wants to control the relationship because women are controlling by nature. It is part of their natural ability as women to organize and raise a family of children.

Her internal nature isn't wrong, it's perfect if she's raising children, but it's extremely destructive to her romantic relationships if its not understood and controlled by the man she's in a relationship with. Why? Because it goes against her ability to stay attracted to her man if he can be completely controlled and manipulated by her wants, needs and demands.

She won't listen to, follow or stay sexually attracted to any man that she can control through his weaknesses because she'll see him as weak. Her attraction to a man is built upon him being a challenge. When a woman doesn't feel challenged by her man intellectually, mentally or emotionally she loses her interest in that man.

He becomes boring, easily manipulated and predictable. This is why she often leaves a "good guy" for a bad guy. The good guy is no fun and the bad guy is all the fun because he stimulates her need for emotional ups and downs. He poses as a challenge for her because he can't be easily manipulated. The good guy is too easily manipulated.

Just ask a woman why they don't like good guys and she'll say quickly "they're boring". So whenever you deal with a woman romantically, you have to always understand that she's looking for her mental edge against you. In the beginning dating and relationship stages, she's always trying to figure you out before you figure out her.

And when you know that from the beginning she's looking for your weaknesses, you can hide any clear weaknesses that you have to stay clear from being easily manipulated and taken advantage of. There are 3 things that you should never share with a woman other than your mom or sister.

Those 3 things are:

1. Past regrets

2. Deepest fears

3. Your insecurities

Most men tell her his weaknesses from the beginning in hopes of gaining sympathy from her, but really you've given away your mystery, given her emotional leverage over you and you've given away your mental advantage to her to use whenever.

A woman will always leverage your weaknesses and use them later as a hot button to push for a reaction when she gets angry at you. This is why you have to stop telling women your secrets and let her tell you her weak areas instead.

For example if you tell her that you have self esteem issues or father issues she'll always use those weaknesses against you when she wants to get an emotional reaction out of you, especially when she's angry and wants you to get angry also. So stop telling a woman everything you feel about yourself and your life, especially negative things that affect you emotionally.

Because she will always use them against you in a fit of rage. By keeping your secrets to yourself you will protect yourself from her trying to ruin your reputation with other girls who gossip. And you'll also protect yourself from her pillow talking with other men to tell your business if the relationship goes bad.

Women Use Your Desire For Sex To Manipulate You

Women like to dominate a man because it makes her feel powerful. Men are in charge in the world, so if she can control and defeat your manhood by using your sexual desire against you, it raises her self esteem and validates her ego to feel power over you.

Because so many men give up the power and control in a relationship in exchange for pussy, she knows her edge is his sexual appetite, which is usually higher in men than women. So whenever she wants to feel powerful or in control of the relationship she simply withholds his access to pussy.

Because she's playing chess while most men are playing checkers. Men play the game for pussy, she plays the game for power and control. Anytime a woman can get you to do what she wants you to do just for what comes freely between her legs, she controls the relationship.

The pussy for her is free, but your power and control as a man have to be earned so it's a losing exchange for you.

Some women try the no sex before marriage manipulation trick to take control from a man from the start. Regardless of what she tells you, it's not because she honors her body, especially if she's not a virgin. It's all about getting control.

She's testing you to see if you're the type of man who will give up your control of the relationship power for sex. She's testing you to see how long you'll stick around waiting to sleep with her. And if she can get you to withhold your desire for sexual satisfaction, she knows that she can control you later in the relationship by withholding sex from you to get her way.

She knows that you will put her into a great position of commitment including marriage, without her ever giving up anything to you of real value. All she's doing is using your lust against you as a stripper does by selling you the fantasy of her pussy for your value. And she's training you from the start of the relationship to put the pussy on a pedestal over your needs and wants.

You give her access to your hard earned resources of time, money and attention, but she gives you very little in return. Because you stayed and took her emotional manipulation, you showed her that you're submissive and easily sexually controlled because of your strong desire for her pussy. Now she knows your weakness and she'll use it for her advantage.

Now she will use the technique of sexual manipulation against you to gain all of the access that she wants to your resources like your time, your money, your attention and your validation, whenever she wants it until there's nothing left to gain. Once she gets all that she wants from you and you have very little if anything left she's gone.

This is how a gold digger works also. The average woman will always try to gain more than she gives from a man even if he has only a little to gain. This is why you can never stay around with any woman who doesn't want to have sex with you in the first month.

If she's attracted to you then it shouldn't even be a problem, because it's a guarantee that she has had at least a one night stand, most women have. When a man has control over his life he can't be controlled by anyone especially a woman.

Because he won't wait for a woman to satisfy his desire for sex while he gives her what she desires, which is his money, his time, his protection and his attention. A weak man is easily manipulated by the pussy because he will give his hard earned money and valuable time for it. But a man who has a purpose and sees himself and his time as valuable won't let pussy control his decisions, ever.

The minute a woman tries to control and manipulate you sexually, it's time to leave the relationship. It doesn't matter how long you've been with her. She's getting what she wants from you, but doesn't see it as important to give you what you want in return, that shows that she's a selfish woman. Never deal with any woman who doesn't see the value in a win-win interaction.

Using Flattery To Stroke Your Ego

Flattery is the excessive and insincere praise, given especially to further ones own interests and ideas. Theres a certain amount of vanity and egotism in everyone. And because a woman understands how to use flattery she easily defeats a man's ego with it. Flattery is the chief bait through which all women seduce men into submission.

She compliments your looks, your body, your great smelling cologne and your accomplishments to open you up to be seduced and manipulated by her. This is how women gain the control over a man she desires, especially men who can't be manipulated through sex appeal alone.

So first she'll try to seduce your eyes by showing her body, and if that doesn't work then she'll seduce your mind through flattery. Flattery is how a woman hypnotizes a man into a web of deception because flattery puts you into a hypnotic state of dopamine highs.

Compliments and praise make a person feel good, and if she uses them properly she can get you to put down your defenses. This is how most men are easily manipulated by women. The lower a man's self esteem is, the easier it is for her to manipulate him through flattery because he's not used to being complimented and praised.

It feels good to have a woman compliment him, so he easily puts his guard down and starts seeing her in the best light. He gets addicted to her praise and then becomes easily manipulated into submission to her, now he'll do anything he can to keep her around.

By using a man's ego and vanity to her advantage, she can win with almost any unsuspecting man without him even knowing. Simply by getting them high with flattery and compliments. Flattery has powerful pulling qualities because it operates through the 2 most common human weaknesses that all men and women have.

<u>Weakness #1</u>: Vanity: The innate desire of all human beings to feel important, have pride in yourself, your appearance, your abilities and your achievements

<u>Weakness #2:</u> Egotism: The outward desire to feel more important, special, unique and better than others to validate your importance in the world

A woman uses flattery to gain an advantage over you so that she can get access to your mind and your inner life. Once she gets access to your inner life then she will automatically earn access to your outer life. That means if she can compliment and flatter you enough to think highly of her, you'll now trust her because of how good she makes you feel.

You won't want the highs you feel coming from her to end. So to keep that source of dopamine "highs" readily accessible to you from her presence in your life, you'll give her access to your money, your time, your body and your attention. This is why any woman who gives you compliments and uses flattery you have to be very cautious of.

Because she knows the power of flattery she has likely used it in combination with seduction on every man that she met before you. So don't let her flattery and compliments go to your ego. It's all just game, never forget that! Even if it's true don't let the high of the compliments she gives you go to your head, stay humble.

Instead, use the art of flattery against her so you're playing the game as the giver of compliments and not the receiver of them. If you can keep this in mind then her flattery and game of seduction through words won't work. The more of an expert you become at recognizing and giving out flattery, the more women you'll be able to get hypnotized versus you getting hypnotized.

Learn how to use flattery in every human relationship you have especially against women whenever possible. This is the only way you can stay away from its effects because you understand its power. Flattery is so powerful that most people don't even see it coming.

So if you're not doing the flattering, then you'll always be a victim to it because it is so addicting and unconscious for most people to recognize. Women are especially vulnerable to flattery through vanity because looks are so important to a woman.

Compliment her hair, her beauty, her clothes, or the way that she wears them, and watch her melt into your arms instead of you melting into hers. Either become the flatterer or be a victim to a woman's flattery. Whenever she starts giving you compliments based upon your accomplishments, your looks, your body or your material things beware of the strategy of flattery!

The Women To Avoid

Avoid The Unhappy Woman

The motto happy wife and happy life is the quickest pathway towards unhappiness and un fulfillment as a man. You're never supposed to live inside of a woman's purpose because most women don't have a purpose in life other than to be "happy". But happiness is not a destination, happiness is a daily task that every person is individually responsible for.

Nobody will ever always be happy and nobody can ever truly make you happy. If a man thinks that his woman's purpose in the relationship is to make and keep his woman "happy", then he is her slave and a slave to her earthly desires and not her spiritual progression which is your real job in her life.

Trying to make yourself happy and keep her happy is an impossible job. Your job as a man is to be the guiding light in her life. Your job is to help her tap into her spiritual gifts, not spoil her or encourage her with the dependency on physical gifts. If you're only focused on giving her physical and emotional gifts you reward a prostitute mentality.

A prostitute only deals with a man by referring to him as a trick. That's because she uses her sex, her eyes, her hair, her body and her mind to trick a man out of whatever she desires from him. Isn't that's all she's using on you as your woman and your wife? What else does she have to offer you in return for being a slave to her needs, desires which she labels her happiness?

Ask yourself, if she left you today what would you miss other than sex and company from loneliness? Nothing! Is it worth being a woman's slave and still rarely getting the sex as often as you want or the things you desire in return? Or are you trying to make her happy, while she sees no benefit in making you happy in return?

Because even if you became her slave and gave her everything she could ever want, she would still end up unhappy because her wants would never end. Your whole life would be built upon making sure she was happy and you would die unhappy. Is it really worth that?

Is dedicating your whole life to making someone else happy worth letting go of your dreams, your desires and your pursuit of joy? Most women will never be happy even if you tried. There's nothing in the physical world that will ever be enough for her to feel happy or satisfied long term.

Sure buying her a gift or you being her slave may give her momentary happiness, but that happiness is simply dopamine released in the brain, not pure and self stimulated happiness that comes from a happy and joyful internal spirit. That's her job to find in life.

There will always be a better purse, better shoes, better clothes even a better man who has more money to buy her all the things she can think she wants more than you could. Her unhappiness comes from her own looking outside of herself for happiness. But happiness doesn't live there, it never has.

Happiness cannot be bought, happiness has to be created internally, that's why so many women don't have it. She has confused temporary "happy" feelings with the lasting joy and happiness that has to be cultivated in your mind through your thoughts of gratefulness, contentment and peace of mind.

Happiness lives inside of your mind. Happiness is a result of having goals, positive visions of your future and a purpose for your life that makes you excited to get up in the morning. Most women don't have that!
If you pay close attention to the modern woman, she has become a slave to media marketing.

The beauty industry, the fashion industry, the entertainment industry and the music industry have all told her that her happiness comes from her buying their products. They have manipulated her mind to be enamored by things outside of herself, instead of the true value that lives inside of herself.

So she gets her hair done, nails done, buys clothes and makeup trying to look pretty on the outside, but never works on her inside. But the more hair, clothes and beauty products she buys and the more her closets fill up with temporary happiness, the more unhappy and empty she feels inside.

As a man, if you believe that you can satisfy the unhappy woman by buying her things and making her life easy by letting her sit home all day without kids, while she sits on social media all day and spends your money, then you're also a slave to the same masters that she has become a slave to.

You've become programmed with the idea that to make her happy you have to do what the media and marketing industry has told her will make her happy. You're a slave to the "happy wife, happy life motto brainwashing. But if these ideas of external beauty over internal beauty they've sold her truly made her happy, why is she still not happy? Why is she still unhappy and depressed?

Why are so many women on antidepressants? Why do women leave relationships over 70% of the time even when they have good and loyal men? Why does she talk so negatively about the men who tried to be what she wanted them to be? Because no man can ever create lasting happiness in a woman ever!

Her happiness is for her to find, just like a man's happiness is for him to find. If he isn't happy based upon his own definition of happiness then how can he guide anyone else towards happiness? How can an unhappy person make another person happy?

Are you a servant and a slave to your woman and everyone around you? Or are you a king who has a kingdom to run and grow? As a man, you can't ever allow yourself to chase after feelings and emotions as the unhappy woman does with her "happiness". You have to be consistent, unemotional and methodical in the process of your progress. This means that you don't have time to deal with an unhappy woman in your life.

She will only serve as a distraction in your life. She will only bring you to your knees mentally, emotionally, spiritually and financially. The unhappy woman will have you searching in the day time with a flashlight looking for her invisible, non existent and ever changing "happiness" with other men.

All you have to do is look around you at the many men who couldn't buy the unhappy woman enough to make her happy. Not even the wealthiest of men could keep her happy, and they have more than enough money to buy her happiness.

Those examples should serve as the proof you need to understand that the happy woman is a black hole for any man who believes he can take on the mission to bring her happiness. You'll do more, buy more, and love more only to find her unhappy with you still. Your purpose in life is never to compromise your happiness for a woman that's already decided to be unhappy.

That's not your responsibility, and it's not a mission that you can ever accomplish without losing yourself and eventually her in the process. Make yourself happy and you'll always win. And the women that you bring into your life, make sure that they're mentally prepared and capable to support the happiness that exists within you. It's the only way that you can avoid the unhappy woman.

Miss Right Vs Miss Gotta Be "Right"

A man will unlock certain things within himself, his mind and his masculine energy when he has the "right" woman in his life to support his growth and his maturity. But when he has miss "gotta be right" in his life she will do the exact opposite. She will destroy his confidence, his self esteem and his vision of his life in the future with pleasure.

The right woman for a man has an inner wisdom within her that upgrades his ability to tap into his highest potential because she adds to his life. She unlocks his heart where he finds a new source of wisdom, knowledge and understanding. The right woman will sharpen a man's logic because she'll say and do things for you that's in your best interest.

She'll say things that enhance your confidence, compliment your character and your masculine energy to make you a better man. The right woman in a man's life has a gift to give him but the miss have to be "right" woman in a man's life has curse words for you. When she's the right woman for you, she's feminine, soft and supportive.

She knows how to plant the seeds in your mind without force, arguments, anger, blame or conflict. And she knows how to gently guide you into a deeper and wiser understanding of things with love. But miss always have to be "right" only knows how to guide through force and conflict.

She wants to force you into understanding with anger and guilt, versus the right woman who guides you into understanding through love and tenderness. Always avoid the miss always have to be right woman because she will torment, complicate, and bring a headache to your life because she likes to fight. Fighting and conflict is an addiction to these women.

And a woman who loves to fight to be right isn't focused on the bigger picture of your vision or the goals of the family, her only focus is on winning the argument, even if that means putting you down and defeating your confidence in the process. She won't stop trying to fight until you submit, even if she's wrong.

This is a prime example of a toxic woman because she will lie, manipulate and even twist your words just so that she can justify in her head doing things that ruin the relationship. Then, when the relationship is over it will always be your fault that the relationship died. She'll never admit her wrongs or accept that her need to be right was the reason the relationship didn't survive.

There's no winning with these types of women, ever! So before you try to fight with miss gotta be right, protect your confidence, your happiness, your reputation and leave while you can. Because when the relationship is over, she'll be determined to ruin your name and your reputation by spreading lies, exaggerations and excuses to why "you" were the problem, not her.

How To Identify A Toxic Woman

Every woman is not for you to keep. While dating, you'll come across women who you're attracted to that are very pleasing to the eyes and the body, but they are toxic and poisonous to the mind of a man. These types of toxic women don't want to add to a man's energy, they only want to take from a man to selfishly add to their energy.

They don't want to be partners and cooperate with a man to create a loving relationship, they want to control the relationship. There are a few simple ways to spot these types of women who are examples of toxic femininity through their actions, behaviors and beliefs about men, relationships and their role in the success of a relationship.

Any woman who first is not happy cannot add to a man's happiness, she can only take from it. If she thinks that controlling the relationship is healthy and that the focus should always be on her happiness, then she's "the" toxic woman. Any woman only seeking to receive and not give in a relationship is like a poison or a cancer to her relationships.

Selfish women are extremely toxic and dangerous to the mental health of any man that entangles his life in any way with her. Here are 10 ways to spot this type of woman. They are qualities of a woman who doesn't care about your happiness, her only focus is on her happiness because she's empty. If a woman isn't happy "before" you meet her, she can never be happy "with" you.

<u>Quality #1</u>: You Are Always The Problem

She never accepts responsibility for disagreements, fights, or arguments, even when she is clearly in the wrong. She'll make you feel like you're always the problem because she never accepts responsibility for anything wrong in the relationship. It's always your fault.

Every time there's a need for her improvement in the relationship, it's your fault she does what she does. She never has to change who she is or how she does things because the only solution to any problem is that you have to be the one to change.

Quality #2: She Is Never The Problem

Anytime you bring up something you dislike to her it becomes an argument or a blame game that's put back on you. Any suggestions that you have for her to improve are immediately rejected. You are always the one who needs to improve, not her.

She doesn't listen to your suggestions or act like she even cares about what you need from her in the relationship. She won't listen to anything negative about her without getting extremely defensive or angry at you for trying to help the relationship grow.

Quality #3: She Gets Upset At Everything

She's very quick to get angry at little things and she becomes uncontrollably angry. She turns little things into big things and you always have to watch what you say to her to avoid a fight or violence verbally, physically or both.

She will throw things, say extremely hurtful words and have no remorse about them. She refuses to calm down and always says that it's someone else's fault she's so angry and upset. She says that "they" made her so angry that she had to react that way.

Quality #4: She Expects Things "Her Way"

You always have to go along with her and do what she enjoys doing and act like you enjoy it, even if you don't. But if you ask her to come along and do what you enjoy doing, it creates an argument and makes it obvious that she doesn't want to compromise at all.

She expects you to always do what she wants you to do happily, but she never wants to do what you want to do without being difficult and showing her lack of enjoyment to ruin your good time. If anything doesn't go "her" way she's upset and angry.

Quality #5: She Controls Your Every Move

She tells you how to dress, what to wear and where you can and can't go. If you do something that she doesn't approve of or she can't go along with you when you go somewhere like with your friends, it always becomes a fight.

If you don't obey her commands or you leave to spend time with friends or family without her, she makes sure that you can't enjoy yourself. She'll text or call you repeatedly to keep the attention on her instead of letting you enjoy your time away.

Quality #6: She Never Supports Your Ideas

Only her ideas are to be accepted and executed. Your ideas are shot down quickly and harshly as not the right ideas. She doesn't trust or validate your ideas or opinions of things because somehow you're not smart enough to make the right decisions.

She doesn't think any business or product you talk about creating will be successful. She always responds with the negative reasons why your ideas won't work whenever you tell them to her. She has no faith that you can be successful at anything.

Quality #7: She's Rude And Disrespectful To You

She tries to make you feel inferior to her by saying things to you that are mean, rude or insensitive. After she says hurtful things to you she doesn't feel bad, apologize or even show remorse for saying hurtful things because she doesn't care.

When you're out in public, she's rude and always talks down to you like you're her son and not her man. She doesn't respect you in the relationship but she expects you to give her respect. Even when she's disrespectful, she expects for you to take it quietly.

Quality #8: She Keeps You Away From Loved Ones

She limits or tries to eliminate your time with friends and family because she doesn't like them for a variety of reasons. She expects you to spend time with her family and friends but she creates a fight when you spend time with yours.

She'll talk bad about your friends, family and your parents to try and discourage you from going places with them. She'll create petty fights, division and drama between you, your family and friends. And she'll try to make you choose between them and her.

<u>Quality #9</u>: She Is Terrible With Money

Regardless of how much money she makes or how much money you give her, she's always in need of more money. She doesn't keep a budget or sacrifice for the future because she spends all of her money as soon as she gets it.

She's never satisfied with the money you give her and she never has enough money to buy what she needs because she spends it so quickly on her wants. So she always needs more money and when she doesn't have any, she always expects you to pay.

<u>Quality #10</u>: She Believes In "Happy Wife, Happy Life"

Her happiness is all that matters and your happiness is secondary if considered at all. She believes that the focus of a man in a relationship is to make sure the woman has everything she needs and wants first before anything.

So you have to always focus on what makes her happy over what makes you happy. If you buy something for yourself she wants to know where hers is at or if you do something for yourself, you're supposed to do something for her also.

Qualities Of A Low Value Woman

The Low Value Woman Is:

- Burdensome
- A Financial Liability
- Arguementative
- Over Critical
- Socially Unaware
- Lacks Communication Skills
- Emotionally Immature
- A Low Wage Earner
- Uneducated In The Basics
- Has A Low Moral Standard

Trait #1:

She's a master at pushing peoples buttons the wrong way. This means that she's excellent at low value attacks or "low blows". She'll get personal and insult the person's looks, character or reveal dirty secrets instead of focusing on the topic of the disagreement.

This go low and attack the person strategy is used to regain control of the argument, instead of focusing on solving the topic and disagreement at hand. She has a very sharp tongue and it's easy for her to say mean things to people without feeling bad about it. And even after the disagreement is over, she's never wrong or the cause of the conflict.

She always has to be "right" and never accepts her wrongs with apologies or by taking full responsibility of her actions. This is a common trait in a low value woman because a low value woman would rather win the argument but lose the man. She's not mature enough to understand that the need to be right is the most destructive force in any relationship.

<u>Trait #2:</u>
She's always unhappy about something because she's always looking for life's imperfections. A low value woman is always looking to change something about herself, but she does nothing about it, but complain. She

really has a low self esteem, but instead of doing something about it like going to the gym and working out, she would rather complain and be insecure about it.

Not only is she highly critical of herself, she's highly critical of everyone else. She's always gossiping about someone else's life and giving her judgements about what they should be doing differently in their lives, but she doesn't put in the work to change the issues in her own life. Everyone needs to change their lives except her.

Trait #3:

She's evasive when it comes to the truth and she never keeps it real, even when she doesn't have to lie. When she gets caught up in a lie she acts very evasive and gets lengthy in explaining herself when she's confronted with the truth. She'll lie just to lie and fool someone because she thinks that it's funny to manipulate someone.

Or she'll lie just to win an argument. She'll use a lie to cover up more lies instead of just telling the truth to come clean and clear her conscience. A low value woman doesn't have a moral compass strong enough to feel guilty about lying because she does it so often. She can lie to others, and she can even lie to herself.

But when she's lied to, she gets extremely upset, angry and talks bad about them as if they're deceitful people. She never considers that she does the same thing to other people and that maybe she was lied to because she lies to them and others.

<u>Trait #4</u>:

She operates a lot in a mindset of shame and guilt. So she talks negatively about herself, her past decisions and her past behaviors because she feels guilty about most of her major decisions in life.

She knows that she hasn't made good decisions in the important times of her life. So instead of moving on and making better decisions in the future, she holds onto the guilt of her past decisions and beats herself up about them often.

<u>Trait #5</u>:

She has a hard time starting something new because her confidence in her ability to learn something new is extremely low. Every time she starts something new, she can never stay focused because her inner self talk is so negative.

Whenever she starts learning about something new that could help her life get better, she gets extremely frustrated and gives up quickly before she can overcome the barrier of frustration that all people feel when learning something new.

<u>Trait #6</u>:

She talks negatively about your plans and ideas of others. She always talks about why your plans or the plans of others won't work instead of encouraging others around her to succeed. Instead of using motivating words and kindness to inspire others to become better, she tries to use guilt and negativity to motivate you or others into action unsuccessfully.

If you do well at something, accomplish a goal or achieve a win that you're proud of in your life, she success shames you in these moments. Her remarks or actions are always negative, sarcastic or condescending, instead of giving you praise and encouragement. She's just projecting her own low self esteem and lack of confidence onto you.

Trait #7:
She uses insults to "put you in your place" under her authority. So she treats you with disrespect and uses sarcasm to lower your self esteem because hers is so low. She'll say smart remarks in front of other people to make you look bad and to try and make herself look better than you.

A low value woman takes pride in her insults and her ability to down someone's self esteem. She likes to insult people instead of inspire someone. Because putting someone down makes her feel powerful instead of inferior to others, which is how she really feels inside.

And she's much more willing to give someone else an insult over a compliment. She insults your weaknesses like your weight, height, money, looks, accomplishments, etc. If you can't take her insults, she'll try and shame you like men should "handle her" and put her "in her place" or he's not a strong man.

Trait #8:
She only cares about materialistic things like cars, clothes, money, her or someone else's educational levels or how much money a man or woman has. She values her life by material things instead of mental things like personality, morals and manners.

She measures a man by what he has, even if she has nothing in her own life. She wants a man that has everything to offer her materially and thinks that she doesn't have to give up anything in the process but pussy to earn his things.

She thinks like a gold digger or a sugar momma who is only focused on money and what someone has. So she idolizes musicians, movie stars, rappers and anyone with money as if they're who she wants to be like or have as a man in her life.

<u>Trait #9</u>:
Low Value women are terrible at:

1. Accountability

2. Honesty

3. Apologies

Low Value women have no self discipline of:

a. Body Shape - She can't push herself to go to the gym to get in shape

b. Her Finances - She spends her money on things that have no real value like expensive clothes and shoes but can't keep money

c. Her Emotions - Her emotional discipline is very low and she can't control her emotions when she's upset

d. Her Mouth - She gets upset quickly and she says inappropriate things at the wrong time. She's always saying things that she shouldn't say out loud

How valuable is she to a man if she:

a. Can't control her finances

b. Can't control her mouth

c. Cant control her mind or thoughts

d. Has no mental order

e. Her surroundings are cluttered

f. Her body shape is not in order

Answer: None!

Masculine Women

A masculine woman is the most toxic form of female because she hasn't learned how two embrace her feminine energy. What makes her toxic is that she's full of resentment, pent up pain, aggression and internal hurt from her past life experiences.

Pain is what made her more masculine energetically in the first place. A masculine woman is simply a hurt woman. So to protect herself from more hurt and pain, she becomes hard in her attitude and very overprotective of her energy like a man does.

Often she'll blame her hard and tough energetic exterior and attitude on the difficult responsibilities of life and her relationships with men, but in reality it's her negative perception of life. Her outlook on life is always negative and made up of a victim mentality. That mentality keeps her from accepting responsibility for her role in the quality of her life.

So because her quality of life is everyone else's fault, she never heals the pain from the past. Because an energetically masculine woman has never taken the time by herself to heal her inner wounds, her wounds are always open and unhealed. So every time someone does anything to hurt her even accidentally, she lashes out to cause them pain.

In reality a masculine woman is a very sensitive and hurt person hiding behind a tough exterior and attitude. She just tries to hide her sensitive self by showing a tough exterior so others won't see that she's truly hurting inside. This is why a masculine woman is the perfect example of the common saying "hurt people, hurt people".

This is why it's incredibly dangerous for any man to deal with a masculine woman regardless of how beautiful she is on the outside. She will only hurt you because she's hurt. And because she hasn't taken the time to heal her own negative attitudes, outlooks and perceptions on life, she can only offer a man her negative energy.

So because her mind is toxic and full of negative energy, she's much more willing to fight than love, and she's more willing to bring your life chaos than order. That's because she doesn't want to cooperate with a man to create peace, she wants to create the negative energies of stress and tension because that's the energy that exists in her mind.

Masculine women bring war and destruction into a mans life. That's because masculine energy by nature is the spirit of competition instead of cooperation. And if she's on the same energetically masculine frequency you're on, then she's a man too. That's the opposite of what creates attraction between a man and a woman.

The magnetic polarity between a masculine man and a feminine woman are energetic opposites, because it's meant to create attraction between them two as different. Two of the same magnetic polarities will always repel each other and fight against each others energy. Just take two magnets with the same energetic polarity, what would they do?

They would repel each other. But if you took two opposite energetic polarized magnets and put them close to each other, they would attract each other, right? Of course! Those two opposite magnetic polarities represent masculine and feminine energy.

A masculine woman by nature is out of her energetic balance and place as a woman when she's in the same energetic frequency as a man. And that's what creates the conflict that exists in her mind, her attitude and her energetic presence in the world.

So she can only bring you conflict because she is in conflict with mother natures order energetically. This is also why masculine women don't like feminine women and talk negatively about them. They see their energetically feminine mothers and grandmothers as weak and submissive.

So they repel and rebel against the idea of being the type of woman that values the energy of a masculine man. The masculine woman has become extremely toxic and negative when it comes to anything feminine outside of her external looks. Any woman who's in her rightful place as feminine energy has become her enemy.

Masculine women see feminine and attractive women as threats because, in reality, she hates anything soft, peaceful, loving, and caring because they represent the balance she is missing in her life. These women are the opposite of what she is supposed to be energetically as a woman. Feminine woman aren't holding onto hurt and pain as she does.

And in her heart she envies their ability to be a woman who attracts the men that she wants. These toxic masculine women will go as far as to chase all the feminine and wifely types of women out of your life. This is also why so many women you meet won't like the energy of you having your mother close in your life.

She'll try to shame you by calling you a "mommas boy" because she doesn't want to compete with any woman who genuinely cares for you, loves you, does for you and treats you in a feminine way like she can't, due to her own inner negativity, hurt and pain. These masculine women can come in the form of your girlfriend, your mom, your sister or your female friends.

They will always chase away feminine women because they expose their lack of femininity. That's because a feminine woman's presence in your life makes a masculine woman feel less of a woman because she is. The masculine woman is out of balance that her natural order mother nature meant her to be in, but the feminine woman is in balance.

So always avoid the masculine woman because you want to only deal with a feminine woman. You want a woman in your life who embraces the gifts of being a woman. Not a woman who wants to act, talk and live energetically like a man, but dress like a woman.

Don't let a masculine friend, sister, mother, aunt, grandmother, etc to push the feminine woman away from your life because they will try. Feminine women are the ones to keep. A masculine woman will never listen to your thoughts, beliefs and ideas regardless of how wise or knowledgeable they are, because they question everything and everyone.

That is her spirit of competition showing. Masculine women want to be the leader and control everything in the relationship because they lack trust in a man's ability to lead. She doesn't like anything that has to do with submission or lacking control of the power in the relationship.

Masculine women always want to argue because they like fighting for power. She loves competing with a man to see who's the most powerful masculine energy in the relationship. That's why fighting turns on the masculine woman sexually because she enjoys the energies of war and chaos.

She gets aroused at the thought of fighting just so she can control you sexually and emotionally to steal your masculine energy. A feminine woman doesn't want to fight because she isn't looking to defeat or challenge you. She doesn't want to compete with you, she wants to complete you.

That makes her feel complete within herself because she is balanced with you around. Some men have made the mistake of having children with masculine women. So they always look to challenge you in parenting styles. She wants to control how you parent, what you say and how you discipline the child.

And if you get separated from a masculine woman, she'll still try to keep her control over your life by creating problems in your new relationship. She'll do toxic things like challenge any woman you date, especially if she's feminine, unlike her. That's why all she cares about when you separate is "Is she prettier than me?"

Feminine women make masculine women insecure because masculine women know that men are attracted to a feminine woman. And because she knows that she can't compete with a feminine woman, she'll try to attack, fight, anger, or embarrass her. Or she'll try to hurt you by restricting your access to your children while she talks bad about you to them.

Feminine women have allowed themselves to let go of their fear of vulnerability and therefore their toxicity. So untrusting, masculine and competitive women want to destroy her with their toxicity by attacking her to break her down. In reality they hate her feminine energy because they know she's better than them at being a woman.

A feminine woman has done what the masculine woman can't do, which is let go of their toughness and take responsibility to heal their pain. All men want a vulnerable woman and masculine women understand this.

That's why they try as hard as they can in the society to tell women they need to be independent, not need a man and keep their focus on making themselves happy, not the man happy. There's a major attack on feminine energy in this society. That's because there's so many vocal and unhappy masculine women who are angry at men because of failed relationships.

Instead of taking responsibility for their decisions in life, choices in sexual partners and their negative masculine energetic frequency, it's much easier for a masculine woman to blame men and say things like "there's no good men", or "men have become soft".

But the reality is men have become much less confrontational with masculine women and would rather cheat or leave than stay in a sexless, emotionless and energetically mismatched relationship, so more relationships are failing. The result has been that masculine woman are more unhappy than ever.

Not because of men, but because their masculine energy has become too much to deal with for a man, especially a man that values his peace. And because masculine women are 70% more likely to leave a relationship because she's cheated or can't find her "happiness" because she's energetically off balanced, most masculine women have a lot of broken relationships.

This pain of another broken relationship only adds to her masculine energetic state. And because they'll blame these broken relationships all on the men, she's left with even more self created emotional trauma. This results in an angry, protective, combative and even more masculine energetic woman.

This is why so many masculine women are usually single, or living with an emasculated man who she dominates. That's why so many masculine women say that "they're happy being single" even when they would easily pick a healthy relationship with a good man over being single and alone.

The truth is that as long as they stay in the energetic frequency of masculinity, they can't do what's needed to give to and sustain healthy relationships because mentally she's not healthy. A masculine woman can't make a man feel like a man because she is one energetically herself.

Only a feminine woman can make a man feel like he's a man because she wants to add to his energy with her nurturing and loving energy. A feminine woman is going to compliment your actions, not critique them. Her feminine energy strengthens a man's ability and his courage to go out and get what he needs from the world so he can share his resources with his woman.

A masculine man is happy to share everything he has with his feminine woman because it gives him joy to see her smile. But a masculine woman wants to take so she weakens a man and limits his ability to truly become his possible self. That restricts his ability to go out into the world and gather abundance that he can bring back to share with her and his family.

And over time she slowly destroys his self esteem and destroys his ego until he becomes a weak and unhappy man. A masculine woman wants your masculinity and she'll do anything to compete and beat you out of it. So you must avoid the toxic masculine woman at all costs if you want to find a good woman in the world. A masculine woman can give you nothing but pain.

The Modern Black Widow Woman

Most modern women have become like black widow spiders. Like a spiders web, the illusion she creates is built to draw you in to keep you from seeing who she truly is until it's too late and you're trapped. A man must always remember that sex and the allure of sex is a woman's most reliable, most effective and most powerful weapon against a man.

The illusion she creates in a man's imagination from wearing tight clothes if any, changing her looks, her body with shape wear, cosmetic surgeries, and using her different costumes is built to lure a man's attention into her web. She lures him in through his sexual desires to steal his life force.

And the men who lack the dick discipline enough to control their sexual desires are like the fly that gets stuck in a spider's web. And as he struggles to break free from the stronghold of the "web"sites, "web" browsers and the world wide "web", ultimately the grip of the web gets tighter and tighter until he physically can't fight his inevitable fate anymore.

He ends up without his life force, which is his inner light. A man's light is the life force he needs to find joy, peace and happiness in his life. His light is what gives him the fire and the desire to achieve success and his purpose in life. A woman understands that the essence of a man is his light.

And once his light is gone, he has nothing more to give her or himself. Like a black widow that sucks the blood out of her prey, there's nothing else left to take once his light is gone. When a man loses his inner light, he loses his desire to exist in the world.

This is why every 13.7 minutes a man commits suicide and men make up 80% of the suicides each year. A man without his light loses his will to achieve. Modern masculine minded women pride themselves on their ability to put out a man's light, but that's because they wish that they were the light.

A lot of females, especially energetically masculine women have a deep contempt and hatred for men. So one way for her to get back at you and other men is to use her greatest gift as a female against you which is her sexuality and her seduction, to put your light out.

A masculine minded black widow woman loves to feel the power of taking your masculine energy. She loves watching you bow down to your lustful desire for her, as she smothers your inner fire through her manipulation of your sexual desire. She loves to see you over value and beg for something that she doesn't see as valuable as a man sees it.

Because her pussy is free and the ability to have sex whenever she wants will never run out for her. Just think of a prostitute. She doesn't value her pussy more than she values money, because money has to be earned.

That's why she can give her pussy up momentarily to a trick for cash so easily. She can even give it up to a man for nothing.

She doesn't value her pussy more than she values money, time, attention or material things, that's why gold diggers and sugar momma's exist. That's also why a woman will never respect a man who pays for what other men get from her for free.

Think of a strip club and how much money women make all over the world simply from selling a man the illusion of him having sex with her. They never get the pussy, but they still give up what they work hours of energy to earn with sweat and hard work. As a man, you'll never gain a woman's respect if she can play games with your mind and body by stealing your inner light.

She'll laugh at you as you trade your valuable light willingly for something she has in abundance for free between her legs. That's why if you strive to become a man of value, you must develop sexual discipline to even stand a chance against the modern masculine black widow woman.

You will never become your highest form of light without sexual discipline and an understanding of what a woman really wants from you. She wants your light because that's what separates you from the black widow woman, that's why she wants it. You have to protect your light with every inch of your inner strength and will power that you have, because it's your life.

You can never trade your priceless light for anything that she doesn't treasure or see as valuable like her sex. Your light is all that you have to combat the darkness that exists in the masculine black widow woman. A strong, disciplined and developed masculine man with his light is the only thing more powerful than her darkness.

Your ability to resist her temptation to steal your light is the only thing that she respects. She respects a man who can't be tricked to follow her sexual advances and trade his light for her darkness. Because only light destroys darkness. The man who protects his light from the seduction of the black widow woman will become incredibly focused, determined and successful in his life.

A man's light is his greatest weapon in the world, just as a woman's greatest weapon is her sexual energy. But the man who succumbs to her temptations will end up weak, powerless and full of regret in life. All you have to do is look at a man before he got into a relationship with a black widow woman and then compare who he is after dealing with her.

See the anger, rage, hurt and pain that's left after she's drained him of his joy, his happiness, his purpose and his light. If you're not careful, she will dim and put out your light if you don't protect your light at all costs. Put your light first, always.

Relationship Addicts

These are women who just can't be alone. They move from relationship to relationship because of their own insecurities and inability to be alone with themselves and their own thoughts. These types of women have a hard time growing because they won't take the time necessary to be alone and heal their present trauma.

Her inability to be alone shows that she's extremely needy and would even choose to be with an under developed man out of loneliness, just to avoid facing her own thoughts. This creates a woman who's always looking to find a distraction from herself and her life choices in the form of relationships.

She would rather try to improve a man instead of taking the time and trying to improve herself. Relationship addicts ultimately become extremely emotionally broken women. That's because each relationship that she gets into, traumatizes her more and more with unhealed emotions, thus creating a compounding effect.

These unhealed emotions become so ingrained into her normal and everyday thinking, that it gets very difficult for her to understand the difference between healthy thinking and toxic ways of thinking. Every relationship that she gets into and then breaks away from just becomes another layer of dysfunction that the other person has no idea comes with her, until it's too late.

Then, when they find out how toxic she is they run. This only leaves her to believe that other people are the problem, instead of her own lack of personal and emotional maturity. The real issue all along was her constant need for relationships, and lack of time for healing her trauma and emotional damage.

The Signs Of A Relationship Addict:

1. She'll stay in dangerous situations just to be in a relationship with someone

2. She thinks her "soulmate" will heal her trauma and heal her soul from its brokenness

3. She can never go without having a boyfriend, a man or male friends floating around her

4. She obsessively doesn't want the relationship to end, regardless of how badly you treat her and she'll do anything to keep it going

5. She's always looking for love in the wrong places that are easy to find men

6. She's extremely insecure in the relationship and constantly needs compliments and validation or she throws a fit

7. She can't maintain any long term relationships because she can't do the hard work when its time to communicate effectively to find solutions

8. She's always looking for the sexual rush of new relationships, so she dresses provocatively to attract new love interests

9. She's always texting you saying "she was thinking about you" randomly, but its really just to keep tabs on you

10. She always needs your attention, especially around others like family or other women she's intimidated by or insecure around

Broken Women

Recognize A Woman's Emotional Thinking Patterns:

a. Look at her past to know her future

b. Does she run to and date mostly broken bad boys?

c. Are all of her past relationships very short?

d. Can she get a man but can't keep a man?

Broken women leave a trail of broken men out of her brokenness. Broken women leaving a trail of broken men are causing a huge issue in the dating market because they leave men hurt, untrusting and traumatized in their ideas about women.

A broken woman expects men to heal her trauma and emotional wounds, instead of her doing her own hard work of healing. But no man can ever heal a broken woman, regardless of how hard he tries to. He will become broken himself by even trying to fix her wounds, because ultimately she'll shut down because her wounds are too deep.

A broken woman has to fix her perception of life to heal her own internal brokenness. Only she can do that work. Because a broken woman thinks that a man can save her from her brokenness, when he doesn't heal her, she runs away to the next man to see if the new man can "heal" her, but he can't either. She just gets more broken in the process of going from man to man.

Broken women use men to occupy their minds, instead of taking the time to heal themselves and their brokenness. So broken women become man collectors and collect each man for different purposes. This is why she keeps other men around. She is broken in pieces and can only share herself with a man in very small pieces.

That's why broken women have a "roster" of men who boost her self esteem, her ego and serve as a distraction from herself and her chaotic mind. Whole women only need one man to be satisfied because she is a whole woman. She isn't broken in pieces because she has gotten herself together and taken the time to heal her wounds.

You can always tell if a woman is broken or whole by paying attention to how many men are around. Does she have a lot of male "friends" and ex lovers in her phone? Does she have to keep in contact with her old boyfriends? These are all signs of a broken woman.

A broken woman is so confused and chaotic mentally, that she will return to the men who bring her chaos and confusion. This is why she returns back to the same broken men and relationships that mentally and physically abused her in the past.

These men are the baby daddies, exes and men who have imprinted her mentally and sexually. These are the toxic relationships she complains about in her past. But broken women will eventually return back to broken men, even after having a good man.

Never try to save these broken women from bad relationships because inevitably she will go right back to the man she complains about. So if she complains a lot about these "toxic" men, beware because she is still mentally connected to them. She blames these men for her brokenness instead of healing her wounds and moving on.

But in reality, energetically, she will always stay connected to the broken man in her past, until she heals herself and lets him go physically and mentally. She will leave a good man with nothing to show for his efforts of trying to fix her out of his love for her. And she will reward the bad behavior of the toxic man with her mind and her body once again.

The more a man tries to pour into a broken woman and heal her brokenness, the more she will become afraid to be vulnerable with him. That's because he's too healthy for her. He's to mentally transparent and direct for her to open up fully to him and fix herself. He's too confident, emotionally mature, too purposeful and logical for her self esteem to take.

This is why broken people and healthy people just don't work in long term relationships. They're too different mentally and emotionally. Internally, she knows that she's unfit for a healthy minded man. She can't live up to his expectations and his pressure for her to open up and grow.

His pressuring her to be open and vulnerable only scares her because she'll have to face the pain of the past. This pressure demands for her to level up and take responsibility for her role in her brokenness, instead of blaming others who can't fix her pain. This pushes her to step up to the plate and be a better woman, but this is always too uncomfortable for her.

A broken woman is not ready or willing to fix herself out of her comfortable pain. She is comfortable not dealing with her issues, regardless of how much she complains and cries about them. She would rather use her pain as an excuse to get sympathy from those around her than deal with them. This is why she will always return back to her "toxic" situations.

She won't be pressured by toxic men and toxic relationships to heal. So she can stay comfortable in her pain and use them as an excuse for her toxic ways, emotional immaturity, and bad relationship behaviors. She may look good on the outside, but you can't always see the brokenness inside her until you get close. You won't know she's broken until you start talking to her.

Life happens to us all, and the world doesn't owe us understanding. We don't get to pick and choose all the things that happen to us. But we do get to choose how we see it, what we learn from it and how we respond to it. Healthy people have painful situations also, but they don't use them as roadblocks to creating a better future.

Broken people will always use their painful situations in life to use as excuses to fight for their inaction. Her complaints about her past and how she's broken because of "other people" is a sign for healthy men to stay away. A woman stuck today in her past decisions is not ready to heal or to take charge of her own healing.

You don't only move forward when things are perfect, you have to move forward regardless. Fear, scarcity, complaints and excuses are clear signs of an unhealthy and broken woman, not looking to heal herself by dealing with her trauma head on.

These women are usually avoiding doing the work because it's an excuse to avoid the pain of healing. A broken woman can get the exact man that she wants, but she still can't handle his healthy mindset when he comes so:

1. She panics and tells everyone he's too good to be true

2. She backtracks and closes up emotionally

3. She leaves because she's terrified

Just Because She's:

a. Beautiful

b. Has a lot of money

c. Educated

d. Has great sex

e. Doesn't mean she isn't still broken

She can have all of these things, but it doesn't mean anything if she isn't emotionally mature enough to handle a healthy man. Regardless of what she "has" or how beautiful she is it doesn't matter. You will become broken trying to fix her brokenness.

She has to do the work and if she hasn't before you, it will never be worth it for a healthy man in the end to keep her. She will always run back to the men that allow her to be broken and don't put the pressure on her to heal and change.

With Toxic Men:

1. She doesn't have to acknowledge and heal her pain

2. She doesn't have to take responsibility to change anything about herself

3. She doesn't have to level up into more of a woman

4. She doesn't have to do the work necessary for healing

5. She can avoid being a better woman with no pressure

6. She can stay in her emotional comfort zone

7. She doesn't have to take responsibility for her role in her trauma

8. She doesn't have to look herself in the mirror to face her emotional demons

A man has to love a broken woman from afar by letting her go. If you're a healthy man, you can't deal with her brokenness. You can't pour into a woman who isn't looking to pour into herself first. Her wanting a man to fix her when there's no way that he can is selfish. Understand it is her responsibility to fix her brokenness.

Your high level of love will only push her out of her comfort zone and back into the arms of broken men. She can have the greatest man on earth in front of her in a relationship, but it still won't turn out well because she's scared to do the work on herself. His healthy mind will challenge her broken mind too much for her to mentally handle.

Broken women sabotage relationships with good men. Simply because she hasn't dealt with a toxic mind and her attraction to toxic men. These women are always waiting for something to go wrong in the relationship with a good man. She really doesn't think she deserves this kind of man internally, regardless of what she says through her lips.

A broken woman goes into relationships with good men already expecting the worst. Already expecting that he will do something wrong to her. This is a huge red flag and a sign that she's broken inside. A broken woman lacks the skills to create long term happy relationships because her overthinking will always get in the way.

She's great at starting a relationship, but she just can't do the work on herself to keep a man around. She just can't keep broken men or a healthy minded man ,regardless of how hard she tries. Unbroken and healthy minded women go into relationships with optimism and are ready to move forward.

Their relationships with healthy men work because they are both two healed and whole people looking to "give" and not "get" in the relationship.When a healthy and whole man loves her in to leveling up, a healthy woman doesn't give excuses. She accepts that he's only building her up into a better woman, not trying to force her to deal with unhealthy hidden emotions.

A broken woman will put in the work to get:

a. An education

b. A good paying job

c. The material things she wants

Yet she won't put in the work to heal the brokenness that keeps her from getting the healthy relationship she wants. Her mouth says she wants a good man, but her actions don't say the same thing. The hardest person for a broken woman to face is the woman in the mirror.

This is her biggest holdup to getting the relationship that she wants. The imprint from dealing with toxic men has become too hard for a broken woman to break. The first man she loved set the standard for her of how love is supposed to feel.

So if her past is filled with toxic and broken men, then this is how she was taught love feels like. She will always feel very uncomfortable with a stable healthy relationship with a good man because she's used to being in toxic and unhealthy relationships with underdeveloped men.

The major imprint of a woman comes from:

a. The first man she loved

b. The first man she had a child with

c. The first man she had sex with

d. The first man she had a big girl relationship with

These men set the standard for her relationship expectations mentally and physically. Her first sexual and relationship experiences set her preferences of attraction and the feelings she's comfortable with in relationships with other men. If you find yourself in a relationship with a broken woman, understand that you're not alone.

There are a lot of broken women out here afraid to deal with their traumas. But you cannot save her emotional life without risking damage to your emotional life also.

Hurt people, hurt people! This is a basic yet very important rule to remember as a man when you're dealing with women.

Avoid Needy Women

It's never healthy for a man to be in a relationship with a woman who is emotionally unstable and needy for attention and validation. It's because she's needy of your energy and eventually she'll drain you until you have nothing else left to give her. This is because her neediness makes her an emotional drain.

That means she's never fulfilled regardless of how much you love, attention or emotional energy that you give her. It's like trying to fill up a big bucket with a hole in the bottom. Regardless of how much you fill the bucket up the hole is just too big to keep the water in. A needy woman is only looking to receive energy.

So because she's always in need of energy, she's not looking to be a giver of energy in any way. That's because inside of her there's an emotional hole that needs to be filled up that she can't fill up herself. That means in her life she's experienced some form of emotional trauma like rape, abuse, abandonment, etc.

Or she's excessively bored, has no friends, has no goals or vision for her life, has anxiety or a very low self perception and self esteem. Because she's always in need of validation from someone other than herself, she uses that person like a child uses its safety blanket. If that safety blanket isn't around, she feels lonely, scared, and now she needs reassurance through its presence.

With a needy woman, you're that safety blanket. And if you're not around to "give' her reassurance and the feelings of safety, she panics and gets extremely needy for your attention and your validation. This means that if you're looking for a woman that can give and receive, then she's the wrong type of woman to be in a relationship with.

She can only give you dependency, she cannot give you the love, trust and freedom that all healthy relationships need. With a needy woman, it's not an exchange of energy like it should be energetically. It's a one person giving equation that will always leave emptiness in the one giving to the needy person in the romantic relationship. And that person will always be you!

The purpose of a man in a woman's life is to be one source of security and safety in her life, not to be her only source of security and safety. She must be able to find her own safety and security in herself first before even getting in a romantic relationship. It may feel good to be wanted by a needy woman at first, but eventually you'll become empty energetically.

That will result in you feeling resentful because she's taking too much energy out of your life and not giving any of that energy back in exchange. And you'll always know when it's time to leave a needy woman because there'll become too much conflict and arguing in the relationship. You'll become uncomfortable and irritable with her excessive neediness in the relationship.

You'll start feeling annoyed at her presence, then you'll start avoiding her. Next you'll have no interest in having sex or spending time with her anymore because her clinginess annoys you. She's taken too much energy and time from you and now you're feeling deficient energetically around her. You have no more energy to give her. This means it's time to leave.

A Lying Woman

A lying woman is an extremely toxic, mentally unstable, emotionally immature and dangerous woman. You must avoid a woman who lies in any way at all costs because she can and will become the downfall of any man that's in her life.

Because She Will:

-Destroy his life

-Destroy his career

-Destroy his character

-Destroy how the world sees him

-Destroy his quality of life all together

Women are believed in modern society much quicker than men are believed. When a woman says a man did something to her, he's guilty automatically before proven innocent by the courts of public opinion. This is why a lying woman is much more dangerous than a lying man.

Women are able to lie on a man and he has to prove that he isn't lying, before he's believed by the public. His character and his reputation will be ruined immediately upon her allegations. Even while he's trying to prove his innocence, he'll still get his character executed in the process.

This is why lying, manipulative, and sneaky women are to be avoided at all costs. So avoid a lying woman completely regardless of how attractive she is, because even consensual sex could become a rape charge. It happens to innocent men everyday! All it takes is for her to be upset at you, or her man to find out about you to put yourself in harms way with a lying woman.

A lying woman will always resort immediately into lying to make herself the victim to get out of trouble and to avoid taking any responsibility for her actions, because that's the way her mind operates. Just one lie on a man can put him in jail and ruin his quality of life forever. She can literally ruin a man with just her words and no evidence.

Because she'll always get the benefit of doubt without having any actual proof of you doing her wrong. Women are much more adept at lying and manipulation than men are, regardless of what society tries to tell you. Women learn how to use emotional manipulation since young ages.

All she ever has to do is cry to get the favor of others. This started with how she manipulated her dad, young boyfriends, teachers, her mother and others as a child. Tears are an incredibly powerful tool for a lying woman because women are expected to cry when something is wrong, a man isn't.

She's learned how to manipulate people with:

1. Her body

2. With tears

3. With victim speech

4. With shame

5. With ultimatums

6. With guilt

If she can't tell the truth, she can't ever be believed because:

a. She's a manipulator and cheater

b. She's an unworthy and deceptive woman

c. She doesn't know how to just ask for what she wants without manipulation

Everything she does is for her own pleasure and satisfaction. She can't be straight up with a man or anyone else. That's because she would rather use deception and manipulation to get what she wants instead of risking the rejection of just asking.

1. This is the obvious sign of a selfish and self centered woman

2. This is the sign of a woman who looks down on men in general as gullible and easily fooled

3. This is the kind of woman who sees men as something to be used and abused instead of loved and adored

A lying woman is a woman never to be trusted because these women don't want a man for the right reasons. They want a man around for their own enjoyment only. And she'll leave you when she isn't entertained or you can't be manipulated anymore. She believes her own lies because she's told so many and can't tell the difference between the truth and the lies anymore.

So she's lost touch with reality because she's told so many lies in her past. Because she's told so many lies about other people to herself and others, she's always the victim in her mind. So she'll demonize everyone in her past through lies and by playing the victim, to make herself seem like the person who was done wrong.

She always uses the victim strategy to avoid all responsibility to change her ways and to avoid just being honest. It's everyone else's fault that she is how she is, never hers. That's why a lying woman is to be avoided at all costs. If you're in a relationship with a lying woman then you will always be the issue.

She'll tell her friends and her family that anything that happens between you two is your fault. A lying woman is an immature woman, in fact, she's not a woman at all! If you value your reputation, your peace of mind, and the quality of your life, recognize you can't change her ever, she's broken and unfixable.

Take your reputation, your value and your manhood and leave, regardless of how much you like her, because you can't trust her. Trust is the foundation to a loving relationship. And respect is it's building materials. If she lies to you, then she doesn't respect you! And if she doesn't respect you, then you have no real relationship.

Most Single Mothers

There's 2 Single Mother Categories:

Category #1: A woman who was married and had a child. She then got divorced or widowed.

Category #2: Women who chose to have a child or more children outside of the bonds of marriage and the child's father isn't directly involved in the home anymore or ever. The primary focus is on category #2 and how it impacts her sexual marketplace value.

The women in category #1 are not the primary focus because they are more responsible than the women in category #2. They at least required marriage. It's the women in category #2 that is the primary focus because she made a decision to have a child, without the demand of marriage before or after.

That doesn't mean that some of this criteria still doesn't fit category #1 also, because it does. A single mother is a single mother. But the thought process of a woman who valued her body enough to require a commitment when having a child shows a higher level of bodily responsibility.

Having a child impacts her value on the open dating market, even if she doesn't want to accept this as fact. All you have to do is ask her if she'll date a man with kids and most women will say no! So she knows the impact a child has in dating.

What most women with children don't understand is that a man isn't just dating her, he's also dating her child. He not only has to win her approval, but the child's approval also. Having even one child extremely impacts a woman's value on the dating marketplace.

Even one child has an impact on her value, just like a man having even just one child impacts a woman's decision to date a man. The fact that she made a child with another man has to be deeply considered in a man's decision to date her.

That's because not only does a man have to contend with her child and the child's acceptance of him, there's the possibility of a jealous baby father. This can be an incredibly bad situation for a man to get himself into, especially if he has no children himself.

That's because that 1 valuable man is getting 3 people or more instead of 1 woman. Instead of him getting 1 woman like he would get if he was with a woman with no kids, that man is getting into a relationship with at least 3 people if she only has one kid.

But if she has more than one kid, he's getting into multiple relationships at once. With 1 kid in this example, he's getting at least 3 people with their own opinions, attitudes, and emotional situations that could cause problems for this 1 man.

He's Getting:

#1. The woman

#2. The child

#3. The baby's father

The more children she has, the more people come in that package just for 1 woman. This is an unfair deal for a man and an incredibly unfair situation for a woman to think a man should settle for when he doesn't have to. 1 man can deal with up to 5 people if she has just 2 kids.

The more kids she has, the worse the deal he gets in exchange for just 1 woman. With her 2 kids that 1 man has to accept maybe 2 baby daddies, 2 children just for 1 woman. That's 5 people in exchange for 1 woman. Does that sound like a fair deal?

This is not what a high value man wants or any man wants, especially if they have other women to choose from without kids. At any time, the child's father can create issues in the relationship and so can the child. A high value man who has other options wanting his attention isn't going to sign up freely for potential problems that could ruin the relationship.

Too many women think that just having one child is no big deal when, in reality for a man, it is. Having just one kid has an impact on his decision to accept a woman, especially if he is a high value man. Your age of having a child doesn't matter. Just because she was young doesn't mean that she can excuse her decision to have a child.

Just because she was young it doesn't matter, she still has a child and that matters. The younger a woman is with a child, it still makes her less valuable on the dating marketplace. This is because a man, especially a high value man, has more young women options without kids to choose from, than women with kids have.

Too many women think that they deserve to be looked at differently than the way they look at men. But how could a woman expect a man to look past what she, as a woman, wouldn't look past herself? That's narcissistic, unrealistic and selfish!

The child is still:

a. An extra expense

b. An extra person in the relationship

c. A third wheel in the relationship

d. An extra person who has wants and needs before her man's needs

e. Connected to another man outside of the relationship

Most women, especially young women, fail to understand that there are women her age to choose from with no children. Why should a man pick a woman with children over a woman with no children with the same to offer? A woman having an outside child is just a bad deal for a man.

One child alone comes with another man as the child's father, who she has a sexual and emotional connection to. A man having to raise a kid who is not his child also comes with extra complications. Getting with a woman who has a child can easily become a parenting problem.

The mother will determine if that man can be in the position as a father role or not. She will dictate how the child is dealt with and how the man can discipline the child. This will easily cause relationship issues because women usually have different parenting values than men in general.

The child will also have the ability to throw the "You're not my father" at any man trying to discipline him when he's unhappy. Just because she has her life together doesn't mean it makes the deal better either. She's still a package deal who brings a man and child along with her. They can always create problems at any time for her, the man she's with and the relationship.

Just because someone is spending money on her and having sex with her doesn't mean that men want her either. Too many single mothers equate a man's sexual attention for his relationship attention. The question is, are the men keeping her after sex when she has a child?

Men will sleep with women they're attracted to, but not see her as wife material if she has children. Because he understands all that comes with women who have children. It's not about her ability to attract a man but her ability to keep a man, especially a man who has a lot to offer other women without children.

Women control access to sex and men control access to relationships. If men are having sex with her but not giving her a relationship in return, they don't see her as wife material, regardless of what she has or how pretty she is.

Her past decisions have consequences and will always impact the men she's eligible for in the world. Just like a man who has baggage or children is less appealing to a woman, a woman with baggage and children is less appealing to a man.

The women that disagree the most will be:

a. The women with a lot of children or who think that "pretty" is all it takes for a man to look past her children

b. The older women who have limited options and less to offer due to a multitude of past bad decisions

c. Accomplished women who think because they have good jobs or money they "deserve" men with a lot to offer

If she wants what she says she wants as a woman, she's going to have to give men what they want in return. Men don't want to raise a child from another man, especially if they have the equal choice to pick women without kids.

Only men who don't have a lot to offer financially or need a place to stay are the most likely to pick a woman with kids. These are the average men that she deserves and not the men with a lot to offer she thinks that she deserves.

Before Dating A Single Mother Ask Yourself...

<u>Question #1</u>: What Is The Family Dynamic?

How well does she get along with the child or children's father? Because the answer to this question will let you see what her attitude will be if you choose to have a child with her. You'll also be able to see her level of emotional maturity by paying attention to how well the relationship works between her and the child's father.

Because the way that she handles the other man, will be exactly how she deals with you if you two separate after having a child together. Her attitude now will be the same with you as the child's father later. If the relationship is too close or extremely volatile, they're both signals of major red flags in the situation.

If they're still very close, then there's a chance she's still in love with the child's father. But if it's very volatile, then the child's father will always serve as an emotional and maybe physical distraction in your relationship with her. There has to be a balance of communication and respect, but not more or less than that in their relationship.

If the child is old enough to communicate effectively by themselves, then all of the communication has to be between the child and the father without the mother being involved. Unless the child can't communicate for some reason or in emergency situations.

Because whenever you have another man who has access to the woman you're with, even if it's outside the relationship, it always has the possibility to create problems for your relationship with her also. This is why the family's dynamics is extremely important for you to understand.

You have to always weigh out if the relationship with the child, the child's father and the mother is healthy or unhealthy. Because if you decide to be in a relationship with her, and take on the parenting role with the child, you are now entering into their already established family dynamic.

Question #2: What Is The State Of The Child's Mind?

Is the child always having issues, or is the child calm and warm. If the child is having issues or is extremely needy of their mother or spoiled, then it will create an issue with the child, allowing you to come into a place of comfort with their mother. A child who's extremely close with their mother may try to purposely create issues by not accepting that mom has a new man.

The child may even go back to their father and create issues with you and the father, especially when it's time for discipline. Understand the mental and emotional state of the child before you get serious in the relationship with the mother.

Because any issues that the child has at home, in school, or anywhere else will become your issues also once you get serious with the mother. If the child is already having problems and issues mentally, emotionally, or both, you're stepping into a dangerous situation, and your presence may make things worse.

Question #3: Does The Child/ren Have Any Relationships With Positive Male Role Models?

Do they have a positive relationship with their father, grandfather, or any other man that they can go to for help mentally, emotionally, or with understanding life in general? Is their conflict already in the relationship with their father, or is their father not even present?

Sometimes the mother can be purposefully trying to sour and taint the relationship with their father due to her own anger towards him. The tension between the parents and the child not having an outside man to talk with will only create a toxic, negative, and bitter environment for the child.

And it will also show emotional maturity issues in the woman you're dating. Never get with any woman who tries to keep her child away from the father or any positive male role models for the child. Because her inability to do what's best for the child only hurts the child in this equation.

A child who's had good male role models around will always be more emotionally balanced than a child who doesn't. That's because they have a positive outlet to discuss their negative emotions. Having a positive man around like a grandfather around will help the child understand that mom is in a new relationship.

If she doesn't have her children around other positive male role models, it's a warning sign that the child is likely emotionally imbalanced. It's also a sign the mother isn't attentive enough to get their child the help they need to mature with balance.

<u>Question #4</u>: What Is The State Of The Father's Emotional Maturity?

Is the child's father in jail, crazy, or present in the child's life? How present are they, and are they already showing jealousy that the mother of his child might be moving on to a new relationship? If the father is present in the child's life, they will tell their father what's going on in the relationship.

There will be no secrets about what happens in the house when they go see their father, even if they only talk to the father on the phone. If there's fights, conflicts, changes or issues with the discipline of the child, they will be discussed and sometimes exaggerated by the child to gain empathy from the father to excuse the child's bad behaviors.

Often times the child will only tell one side of the story to make themselves the victim and manipulate both sides. If the father is emotionally unstable or violent, this is a dangerous situation to put yourself in because it could get you hurt or killed. More often than not, the child will only tell their father one side of the story as a form of emotional manipulation.

A child does this so that they can make the father mad enough to defend the child. This is another reason why it's so important to pay close attention to the emotional maturity level and behaviors of the child, before you get serious about any single mother.

Also, if the child is good at manipulating these situations, it will cause issues with you and the mother also. This could result in the mother and father teaming up on you and making you the bad guy, which could be very dangerous to you.

<u>Question #5</u>: Is The Woman Bitter At The Child's Father?

If there's bitterness, then she will always try to make him jealous of your presence. She will use you to make him feel inadequate, obsolete or envious because she's still not over him fully. If she's not over him, then he will always have access to her emotionally. This will result in him causing her to be angry, upset or emotionally off balance.

This will disrupt the flow of the relationship and distract her from what you're building together. If he knows that she's still mad or bitter at him, he will use it to create problems and issues in the relationship for his own amusement. He won't let her move on in peace because he knows that he can manipulate her emotionally.

And because she's still emotionally tied to his thoughts and opinions of her, she will respond to his feelings and actions of distraction or disrespect with anger, sadness and resentment. If any woman you seek to deal with isn't over her ex and talks negatively about him in an extreme way then she's not over him.

You want a woman that understands what he's done wrong and is ready emotionally to move on. But more importantly, she accepts what she's done wrong that resulted in the failed relationship. If he did all the wrong and she did nothing wrong in her eyes, then she's still not over him. And she's still not ready for a healthy relationship with a new man.

A woman who's emotionally tied to another man still has her heart strings attached to that man. All it could take is for him to show his remorse or for him to try and get back with her in any way and that would complicate or end your relationship with her.

<u>Question #6</u>: How Well Does The Mother Discipline The Child?

Is she extremely lenient, afraid to hurt the child's feelings, lacks the desire to discipline the child, or she allows the child to say whatever and be disrespectful in any type of way to her? Does she guide her child through talk first, or does she spank the child over small things and get extremely angry at the child over small things like small mistakes?

How well does she handle herself when it comes to her child's defiance? Will she let you have the ability to discipline the child? Or does she think that you can act as the position of the father, but not have the rights to discipline the child as a father?

A woman who won't allow you to discipline the child will show the child through her words and actions that your words are not valid and valuable enough to be respected. This is a big problem! Because her disrespectful actions towards you that she shows the child, will only create division in the relationship between you and the child and also between you and the mother.

If you cannot take on the full role as the father figure in the home, then you're guaranteed to have issues with the child saying you're not their father along with the mother saying the same. You will have no authority to be a balanced figure in the home. Because you will always be expected to give money, time and energy, which will ultimately be thankless.

But you won't be able to give the child the balance of love and discipline a child needs. Or if you're expected to discipline the child only the way the mother sees fit, then she will always criticize the way you discipline the child in front of the child, which will always ruin the relationship. Eventually they'll just team up against you as the bad guy.

Because the child will be able to very easily manipulate a wedge between you and the child's mother. Any woman who doesn't agree with the way you discipline the child, will always go behind your back and give the child whatever privileges you're trying to take away. They will always sneak behind your back and allow the child to undermine your authority, just to make the child happy.

Therefore, putting you in the position as the "bad guy" and the mother as the "good guy". If the parenting values and discipline techniques between you and the mother are different, then you must get away from that situation immediately before it gets unhealthy because it will.

Differences in parenting values is the most common enemy to a healthy co parenting relationship. This is why it's so difficult to be with a single mother. Because the way that she disciplines the child is the way the child is used to being corrected.

Any other type of discipline will be rebelled against, especially if the child is a girl. A daughter will always take the side of the mother, especially if the mother doesn't stand by your words while you discipline the child.

The child must always see a united front when they see you and the mother. Any type of division between you and the mother will be taken advantage of by the child. Because all the child has to do is manipulate the weakest link in the parental relationship.

The Social Media "Model"

Her energy is built to drain you of your energy by using your desire for sex to manipulate you. So she lures a man in and then uses for herself his emotional energy in the form of his attention, which drains his physical energy, his sexual energy and his physical resources.

Qualities:

1. Non submissive

2. Domineering

3. Controlling

The Men She Looks For:

-Weak men who are easy to manipulate
-High powered men
-Men in high positions

-Men with fame

-Men with power

-Men with money

She uses flattery and seduction to lower his defenses because she seeks to establish emotional, mental and sexual control over men so she has full access to his physical, mental and emotional resources. She surrounds herself closely with weak, submissive and vulnerable men who validate her often with sexual and emotional attention as old friends, fans, exes, etc.

She keeps these men around on social media, at her job in the form of work husbands, in her phone as phone husbands and in church as church husbands. Having these outside men around makes her feel like she has options over you. This also serves to make you submit to her through using your jealousy and insecurity against you.

So she'll have male friends around on purpose to make you jealous. But she'll act like you're being the jealous one for no reason. This type of woman is increasing everyday as women become more and more addicted to social media. A woman can take pictures of herself and get the attention now of men all over the world.

This is a kind of power that women have never felt before. This is extremely toxic for healthy relationships to exist because it's extremely tempting for her to look in her dm's and find a man who has more money, status and attention to offer her. A woman you find on social media looking for the attention of men is an addict.

She's no different than a drug user because social media attention releases the same dopamine chemical to her brain and gives her a temporary emotional "high". If you find her on social media, especially dressed in revealing clothes, leave her on social media.

Once she gets used to the "high" of social media attention, there's no way that your attention can compete with the highs the attention of different men give her. Once the high of your attention gets old, she'll return back to her social media attention fishing ways. Most women have low self esteem.

But now all she has to do is turn on her phone for a quick fix of self esteem even if it only last 5 minutes. You or any other man will ever be able to compete long term with the algorithm of social media. She'll put on more and more revealing clothes and take more revealing pictures to fulfill this "high" until she becomes like the next woman in the next chapter.

Leave Porn Stars & Strippers Alone

<u>Reason #1</u>: Women in the sex industry have seen too much of a man's vulnerability to sex. So her image of a man is tainted to one of untrustworthiness and disloyalty anytime she thinks about men and her in serious, monogamous relationships. In the sex industry, she's exposed to mostly men whose focus is only on sex, so she thinks this is how all men think.

She's been trained to think that's she's only good for sex, so internally she'll battle to find her importance in a relationship with a man. She has no faith in men because all she's seen are perverted men. So she doesn't believe that men are good in general. Even good men are labeled bad in her eyes because they just want sex in her mind.

<u>Reason #2</u>: She's used to dealing with men willing to compromise their values and part with their valuable possessions for sex. So she'll have a hard time seeing you

as her man and not a "trick". She's used to using pussy as her tool to get what she wants to manipulate a man.

So she will always resort to sexual manipulation whenever she can't get her way with you because it's worked so well in the sex industry. These women just end up dealing with sugar daddies and not husbands because she can't trust a man to be loyal to her even if he is.

Her mind has seen too many more low quality men to believe that men want her for anything other than sex. So she finds it much easier to deal with men that she knows what they want, like sex, instead of relying on her trust that a man really desires her more than just her pussy.

Reason #3: She will always be afraid of a real relationship because it's so hard for her to accept the idea of a "good" man. She's never been exposed to one in the sex industry that she works in. She's ingrained with the idea that all men are cheaters, and that all men can be easily sexually manipulated by a woman.

So she fears that just like she's manipulated men with sex, another woman will come along and manipulate the man she's with, sexually. She has likely seen married and committed men compromise his values to have sex with her or others. This destroys the idea and image in her mind that even men with beautiful women and wives at home are good men.

<u>Reason #4</u>: She's addicted to the attention of being admired lustfully. Because she's so used to being admired sexually and given so much attention by men, she craves it. This will urge her to flirt and be more sexually seductive, even with men she isn't attracted to because she likes feeling desired by men.

She's very good at seduction because she's made a living out of it. She can be very seductive without saying a word. It makes her feel powerful to be lusted for and given sexual attention. So when she doesn't get that type of attention from you anymore, she will use your friends and other men in her direct circle to get this attention.

<u>Reason #5</u>: She's likely a victim of sexual abuse. Often, women in the sex industry are victims of rape, molestation or other perversions. This is often the catalyst for her over sexual behavior. Sexual abuse creates a woman with emotional, mental and sexual damage.

And a woman who is damaged mentally, emotionally, and physically will always have barriers up when it comes to being open enough to accept love. That's because she has internal trust issues that aren't easy for her to move on from.

These issues will always show up in the relationship when you least expect it and cause emotional bonding issues. You can't create a deep emotional connection with a woman who has internal trust issues and damage to her psyche.

She will always do something to sabotage the relationship when things are going well because she thinks things are going too well. She just can't accept that she's worthy of being loved. She sees herself as damaged goods. And because she sees herself as damaged, she'll always have a hard time accepting that a man truly loves her and won't hurt her.

<u>Reason #6</u>: She very likely has daddy issues. Women in the sex industry are often the result of being raised with single mothers, drug addicted mother/fathers, no fathers, foster homes or mothers in the sex industry. So because her parental life and environment were so bad, often these women do not have strong family support.

She craves the guidance and strength of a father so she often deals with men who have father qualities but still see her as a sexual object. This makes her feel even more lonely because the connection of a daughter and a father has nothing to do with sex, but love. The environment she's in makes her daddy issues worse because these men only look to take advantage of her.

Reason #7: She likely has drug problems and issues with alcoholism. The sex industry lifestyle creates a lot of stress, guilt and shame that most women cope with by using drugs and alcohol. Drugs and alcohol go hand and hand with the lifestyle.

So over time, it creates a habit of unhealthy substance dependency behaviors that push her to rely on these addictions just to keep doing what she's doing. The feelings of shame and guilt add up in her mind, so she needs more and more drugs and alcohol to cope with these feelings.

All of these feelings and reasons compound in her and make her unworthy of a real relationship or a healthy connection with any man. Her psyche, her body, and her subconscious is too ruined for her to be able to pair bond with a man. Just having too many sexual partners alone ads up inside of her womb to make her spiritually unable to really connect with a man to take seriously.

Rebellious Women

If she doesn't appreciate wisdom, leave her to foolish men. There's only two types of women in the world, the wise woman and the foolish woman. Her desire for wisdom is the only trait that separates one woman from the other. So if she doesn't respect wisdom then she's the foolish woman who doesn't listen or respect anyone.

A woman who doesn't listen or respect anyone has no mental discipline. So she'll never even listen long enough to accept a man's point of view. So until she respects wisdom she's not worthy of a man. These women respond to your wisdom with negative opinions and emotions like anger, shame, and blame, which are all rebellious behaviors.

A rebellious woman with an opinion about everything, will never state facts, literal or physical examples or actual truths about a disagreement. She'll only talk about "her feelings" and express emotions. She'll never just do what you ask her to do without always thinking twice about what you said.

A woman who thinks that she knows twice as much as you doesn't respect you, so she'll always question what you have to say. She'll go left when you tell her to go right. Because when a woman thinks she's mentally, spiritually or physically stronger than you, she will always test your mental and physical strength.

This rebelliousness in a foolish woman won't even submit when it's obvious that you're right. Why? Because she doesn't want to give you any feelings of power over her. Because every time she beats you at something, especially mentally, she feels more powerful than you. She likes the feeling of beating a man at something and it inflates her ego.

If you have a woman who likes to out talk you, she enjoys verbally sparring with you because she wants to beat you mentally. She thinks she's smarter than you.

Most women will choose the mental battleground with a man because she thinks its her advantage over a man. She knows that the physical battleground is most likely where the man has his advantage.

Any woman who like's to verbally fight with you will never listen to you. She'll always listen to her emotions and the rebellious thoughts in her head, instead of your wisdom. A rebellious woman doesn't like listening to any wisdom and logic or to be given direction, even if it's good direction.

These women have usually been rebellious since they were children. They rebelled against their parents, authority figures and anything with rules. So to her, she sees a man giving her direction and wisdom as control. She doesn't see it as guidance, help and some logical direction for her undirected mind. Her inner feelings are always to rebel against anyone trying to give her positive words.

The only women who respect wisdom and knowledge, are the women who possess it themselves. The wise woman will listen intently while you speak because she respects your wisdom. Her ability to listen inspires your ability to listen. This is the only type of women you want to seek as a man. Who you connect your life to is incredibly important.

Too many men have connected their lives with unhappy women who can't add to their ambition, success, goals or their energy. The goal is to become the best man you can be, extraordinarily. Women have a place in your life, but they can't be #1 over you, your health, your goals, your dreams and your plans in life. A man has to have a plan. If you lack a plan, you're not a man!

Enjoy The Wisdom Contained In This Book?

For More

@theministerofmanhood

All Wisdom Works If You Work It!

If You Received Useful Tools In This Information, Please Give Me A 4-5 Star Rating!

This serves as a reward for an author. It takes hours and months, sometimes years of no pay to put together books for the purpose of sharing information you see as important to the world.

Please just take out a minute of your time and please leave a quick positive review. If you didn't receive any value from this book then dm me on instagram @theministerofmanhood to tell me why.

Either way, Thank you tremendously for taking out the time to read this information and knowledge. If you really took this information seriously and you applied the key principles into your daily life, I KNOW you are seeing results.

So again, I thank you for your interest in learning and any investment in applied knowledge will always be a winning investment.

THANK YOU FOR READING

NOTES

www.ingramcontent.com/pod-product-compliance
Lightning Source LLC
Chambersburg PA
CBHW050313160726
48002CB00001B/16